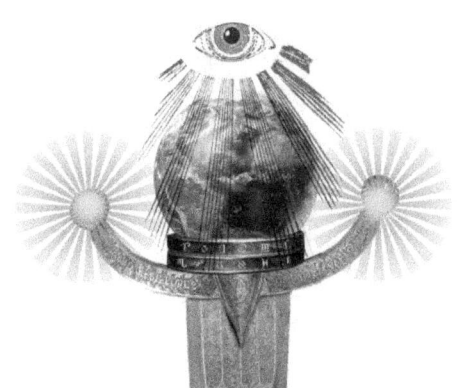

NATURE'S OUTLET
~BEHOLDER OF THE GRAIL~

Le Roy Walker

NATURE'S OUTLET
"BEHOLDER OF THE GRAIL"
by LE ROY WALKER

ISBN: 1519770928
ISBN-13: 978-1519770929

CONTENTS

"INTRODUCTION TO THE DOWELS"

Greeting Everyone!

I have something I want to discuss with everyone. This book is a discourse of my knowledge and experience and is chosen as a medium to reach the interested audience around the world. This book would unfold as a lecture about life and truth and is an attempt to enlighten the inquisitive and curious minds, with a desire to explore the ultimate truth about the world. As a part of this lecture, you would get a chance to examine yourself by acclaiming truths about yourself. You would be asked to explore your personality by listing down your strengths, weaknesses, positives and negatives. The exercise would be an attempt of self-evaluation, where you acknowledge your selfish desires, and assert the definitive truth about yourself. Let's call this document the "*ultimate document of self-truth*".

"*The ultimate document of self-truth*" is intended as an organized guide that would help you to engage in thorough self-analysis and to make confessions to yourself. My lecture would be supported by a set of activities aimed at increasing your awareness about yourself, improving your communication skills and recuperating the outcome of your actions. The exercise would help you become aware of your emotions at conscious and sub-conscious levels and would enable you to draw up a plan of action for targeted personal development. The objective of this training is to spread my knowledge of self-efficacy among all of my readers so as to guide the humanity on the part of righteousness. This manuscript is a small personal attempt to preach life lessons to my followers; however, I can also be approached directly for advice and help through email and by my official website. I am a humanitarian, I love mankind and therefore, I am resolute to explain the true meaning of life to my followers and to help them solve the difficult situations of life by becoming directly available to them. My endeavour to help and guide the humanity is selfless. The reason behind my work is to explain the *secret monopoly* of this world to the entire human race. This hidden monopoly possesses the ultimate power to influence humanity and the details of it would be explained later in this book.

By the time I am finished with the laid down activities; you will be at a higher level of self-awareness and would be fully acquainted with your needs and wants. This is the point where I would like to enlighten you about the methods of healing one-self by using natural methods to reincarnate the facilities of your very own existence. I will be making use of my own personal experiences, to teach, and also to give examples. I have laid down some universal methods to benefit humanity, and I do suggest that everyone make use of these methods which have been provided below under the section of "**sacred numbers**".

Human Dowel: There are several types of human dowels, including; mental, spiritual, emotional, and the physical dowels. These terms, taken together are known as the "*Dowel pulse*" which ultimately represents the Human Soul. It is vital to note here that some people are mentally strong, but emotionally weak; whereas, others have a strong spiritual sense with physical weakness. It is significant to comprehend that every human is a unique mixture of these dowels with varying strengths and weaknesses and the book would go on to individually address these dowels.

The Mental Dowel

1st Law- The Mind (*which is you*): The first law declares mind as an objective machine and urges you to not to follow it exclusively. Mind is known to have mechanical tendencies with a function to create, learn and store things and to make observations and proper recognitions for the purpose of future references. Mind/ You act as a magnet among all the objects that are around you and therefore human beings are known to have absorbent tendencies, since they pick explanations and meanings from their surroundings. A human is intelligent since he has a receptive mind and the human body serves as a home for this mind. It is said that "Body is mortal but great minds are eternal". However, mind, only when treated as an organ of the body is perishable; whereas, a *human soul* is everlasting.

2nd Law- You as a part of Greater Whole: You being a "Mind" must understand that you engage with, interact to and learn from other people or other "Minds". In easier words, you are a part of a greater whole.

3rd Law- The "Dowel Pulse": *Which is You (as the energy, and the intelligence):* In order to polish your personality and to get the best out of your abilities, you must *add* all of these laws to have an intrinsic understanding of your personality and to make right choices on the daily basis. These laws, taken together would make you "self-disciplined" and would make your actions more focused and abstemious for streamlining your daily life.

"The Inductive Power of the Mind"; - is vital to gain calculative control on your body and to monitor your actions. If you would be more aware of your daily actions and would take well-thought, anticipated actions, you are more likely to be successful in your lives. By using the inductive power of your mind, you can perform the following essential functions;

"**Observance**"- Observe the situation in which you are in, before you make a judgement about it, or proceed with an action.

"**Research**"- Make it a practice to gain sufficient insight into a subject matter before you do "deductive reasoning". Research thoroughly and then claim to know the details of the subject concerned.

"**Stay Focused**"- Focus and concentration are the off-shoots of patience and determination. Be very aware of your surroundings and "*mentally*" place the relevant pieces of information together to form as "informed" decision. An objective decision can only be made if you use your common sense, pursue your intuition, use your positive energy and take into account the warnings and signs of the nature To sum it all up, you need to balance your reactions to the actions of the mother nature, so as to become wise and have harmony in your life.

"**The Emotional Power of the Mind**"- Emotional power of the mind helps in;

"Emotional attachment": Emotional power of the mind is a guide in learning of, as to how to take care of and show respect to the people we care about. It determines our body language and helps us to communicate gestures without words.

"**The Physical Power of the Mind**"- The physical power of the mind indicates the thought process behind every human thought; let it be big or small. It is important for my readers to understand that the physical power of the mind cannot defy the parameters of universal truth since 'Truth will always stand, for it is invincible, and shall lead the future and follow the past'. The human thoughts, would therefore, be always leaded by the truth.

"**The Morality of the Mind**"- The mind shall follow the basic principles of morality, in order to grow and learn from the surroundings. Under the command of morality, it would perform the following vital functions.

The mind shall stay alert and focused to the elements which makes it stronger, helps it to grow in potential, as well as, in capacity. It will be strengthened by imparting knowledge to others. The morality of Mind is bounded to the fact that the human mind has selective retention. It will absorb only those facts which make it stronger.

The mind shall cope with and acknowledge to the principles of *'righteousness'*, which can only be achieved by moulding the persona through all the above stated "*Dowels*".

A wise and ethical mind would reject ignorance, thoughtlessness, inanity and unmarked pleasures. *Unmarked pleasures* can be defined as those pleasures which have not been fulfilled through legal, honest and truthful ways.

The Mind shall figure out ways to complete

important tasks in time, by breaking habits of procrastination and ill-management. A mind rich with morality would try to overcome harmful habits and would try to defy laziness, denial and indolence. For positive and productive physical outcomes, the power of the mind has to be constructively utilized to get the desired results.

MENTAL WOES:

The following sources of mental despair are to be avoided at all costs to have a positive personality;

Do not welcome acknowledgements that are not relevant to your personal value. Avoid flattery and mentally strive against "sweet words which are meant to falsely gratify and please you".

Do not lie to yourself. Admitting truth with self is the first step towards self-actualization.

If you fall for the above two "forbidden" evils, your spiritual decay would soon be inevitable.

Pertaining to the above mentioned points, one must observe, recognize, and acknowledge, before claiming to be "All-Knowing", (and I repeat that sometimes this take patience),especially when you are on a journey to deconstruct your old self and re-construct a new self; like right now.

It is also vital to realize that people who claim to

be self-righteous, or have a tendency to beat you down with the false deception of their experience, are you enemies; especially when you are on a journey of Spirituality. They would make attempts to break you down "emotionally", "spiritually" and sometimes even "physically" by inducing the negative elements of doubt, temptations and fear, inside you.

Remember my dear students; it is significant for each one of you to master the knowledge about all Dowels, before you proceed with the applicability of them in your everyday life.

I would begin the lecture by explain the laws of Dowel, which would eventually help you to understand my point in greater detail.

The Law of *Emotional Dowel*:

"Emotional Dowel", is the gift of the nature to human beings which is naturally assorted with the components of all other Dowel, explained later in detail. Emotions are a blessing of nature since they make you aware about your surroundings and help you take difficult decisions of your life. My dear friends, the Dowel Pulse, is guided by your inner most emotions. Emotions, in turn facilitate you to gain intrinsic awareness which helps the "invisible vapours" of the Dowel Pulse (The Soul) to be on the right path.

The mind, with the help of intelligence, is only capable of the mechanistic functions like growing hair and nails, maintaining an immune system and producing heart beats. It does not help you with intuition or insightfulness into the matters, since it is devoid of emotions. But if the mind is used objectively (as a Brain), utilizing its all other processing tools (like thoughts, observation, perception and acknowledgements), it can be greatly valuable for you. It must be realized that since truth is invincible, the human mind must be able to acknowledge it, even before it has fully materialized to its tangible existence.

My dear students and friends, it is important to know that in order to gain a dominate control over the self; you need to have full knowledge about you. Make attempts to seek all truths so as to grow into a disciplined, wise and honest human being. A strong person is the one who shuns all his negative energies by staying away from the evil acts. He practices self-restraint and does only the right things. He has full control over his words and actions and does not let an emotional storm to sway him with it. Therefore, being my students, you must realize that the more patience you have, the more you would be able to control your actions.

Let's talk about *Emotional intuitions* now. Being a human and a social animal, connected with people and situations, you need to make a lot of decision and vital judgements on daily basis. Your intuitions are a guide for you while you make these choices. A brain with its intelligence, memory and the storage capabilities of your mind, together with your emotional intuition help you to have an informed living. Your spirit is in direct contact with your emotions. The more positively and realistically fuelled your emotions are, the more stridently your spirit would radiate positive energy. This would mark the beginning of a "*Spiritual Era*" for you. With the tools of your mind being parallel with your positive emotions, your soul would be strengthened with healing light. This positivity would eventually be reflected by your physical appearances of calmness and a happy demeanour.

I would now like to shed some light on the Emotional traits. They are love, hate, happiness or sadness and are expressible. They can also be reflected, in physical form, as *Acts* in the life of other individuals. Besides emotions, another important chord, tuning the lives of the individuals is their 'intentions'. Your intentions dictate your actions. There is a momentous quarrel of good or bad intentions going on inside every human being. As a Human, you are being graded by your own Guardian energy, which is being lighted by your own actions and reactions. It is important for all of you to realize that spirit and mind (*meaning you*) does all of the shifting, and allowances of the spiritual, and physical expressions. The mind also reveals what is being determined, through the spirit, to be given, unto all others.

As a student of the lessons in this book, you must know that you being a human, you can easily become over-ruled by only one of the Dowel, rather than having a propionate balance of Dowel impulse in them. For Example, it is largely possible that you are mentally strong but physically weak; you may be spiritually gifted but emotionally feeble. This, by no means determines, whether or not you are strong as an individual or not. The dominance of one Dowel over the other is influenced by several *factors* like your physical surroundings, your age, your personal interaction with people around you and the choices you make in life. These aspects, taken together and the World, in which we dwell in, make us who we are today. However, it must be noticed that every human can bring in emotional improvements in them by trying the following *emotional enhancements*.

Emotional Enhancements:

Everything that is striven, to become a reality, from such an individual, must have a good truth, and meaning, for the better of one's life, as well as for the need, of someone's else lifestyle, .

For the emotions run deep, and is personal, which beholds greater, and lesser situations, by expectations, that varies, amongst physical choices, determined to be made, by such an individual, "EMOTIONALLY"

Emotional Woes:

The Emotional Woes have been listed below for your reference;

The emotional distress is mainly the result of lack of control over mind, the inability to maintain the peace inside you and the lack of emotional knowledge. Becoming emotionally intelligent by defying your fears and doubts and by having high hopes would grant you spiritual relief. It would keep your mind stable and would free you from the needless worldly worries. Having positive thoughts and by realizing personal strengthens, the subject would feel good about himself and would be emotionally stable with an instinct feeling of peace. This would in-turn boast the confidence of an individual and would improve his work productivity, which would indirectly boast his self-esteem.

"The Laws of the Spiritual Dowel"

The spirit would only house energies from emotional trades, such as interactions, imaginations, and even creative ideas; that are spiritually inculcated and feed emotions of a human being. The Soul radiates the type of energy which has been passed on to it by your personal interactions and your conduct, whereas, your spirit (which is the energy inside of the body, being you) records and stores all that had been passed down to it, in order to spark a reaction from you.

Example of a lesser key, on this subject:

Tony met a boy named James one day at a park.

They have been friends ever since, and the more they hang around together, the closer they get to one another.

Now a lot of emotions have been exchanged between both of the parties, as time passes by.

Since a lot of time has passed of them being together as friends, Tony cannot recall all the minute details of his conduct towards his friend, neither can he recollect the particulars of all the joyful moments they had together. However, he is aware of the fact that they have been through a lot together. So, when he speaks of his companionship with him, he speaks from an emotional angle, which is connected to his spirit, since it is the spirit which maintains the inventory of the emotions.

The learning from the above given example reveals that once a person has forgotten the specific details of an act or about a person, the energy associated with that act still persist and help a person to form an opinion or adopt an attitude towards a situation or towards another human being.

This is true for every relationship. If spirituality is to be treated as the face of our everyday life, the emotions would be the tongue.

All acts, being up raised, by the deeper emotions, are to be placed, within the spirit, of a human's existence. That it may be repeated by the subject, in its lifetime, as a habit,(which also may include the risk, of family's inheritance, of such an act, being spiritually passed down, to the subject, that is in the physical form, with us all, today.

For the spirit is the essential glue, for all other dowels, to stand in its truths, as well as belief, faith and deceitful matters.

All depending on the choice maker, in the physical terms, of reality (which is "YOU").

It must also be noted that even thoughts and perceptions of the mind, the dreams and nightmares and all the spiritual assets (controlled or uncontrolled) by the individuals.

Soul in itself is a spiritual being so "You" do have a spiritual existence as well.

In order to reveal your true identity, you must get

familiar with your *spiritual realm.*

Spiritual enhancements
The spiritual guidelines have been listed below;

Picture positive things in your mind which provide you with intrinsic peace and comfort, while you perform good deeds in your environment. This would help you to witness the beautiful mist of your spirit, would grant you happiness and would help you dwell in harmony.

Follow people who have a positive spirit. Following an aggressive person, with violent propensity means following a negative spirit. Although, it s true that every leader is a follower of some kind and every follower has some leadership tendencies. A person with positive spirit would always have a higher standing in the spiritual realm.

The above discussion brings you upon a single point of contemplation i.e. "who you are going to choose as your leader?" You must be lead by someone, who operates at the same spiritual frequency as you do. It would help you to maintain your intrinsic peace. Using the tools of mental intelligence, intuition and the right portion of positive emotions, you must only accept the right information from your leader. In case your leader has an unpleasant presence, which imparts disagreeable messages, you must be able to block the negativity of it, by using the power of your Dowel Pulse. It should be noteworthy that your boss or your leader would always have several things to offer to you, let those things be material or immaterial, but the responsibility of choosing only the right offerings fall upon you; since the Dowel Pulse would always be your guide, if properly understood and applied. Common sense, being a sub-branch of Dowel Pulse is a natural guide for human beings, when they engage in interactions with the fellow humans.

The advice to choose the right leader, does not, by any mean signifies that you must judge or label others or consider them as inferior beings than you are. It only signifies that using the power of your "knowledge" learned from this book, you must always create a positive context around you. You must be equipped with sufficient understanding of all the situations around you and using the information imparted by this book, you can look for good things in all scenarios. The best way to get acquainted with the underlying truths of the world and in order to gain full control over yourself, you must practice meditation. Meditation is a form of long-thoughtful process that allows a human to ponder over the hidden truths so as to get answers for his awareness. The truth is indomitable and pursuit of truth would help you conquer the wonders of the world.

The details of the Spiritual woes have been listed below;

The negative feelings or the sentiments of hatred towards another human being are the results of your value judgements, poor ability to form an opinion and the failure to realize the contextual situation of the person in question. Sometimes, the hatred is induced inside you by another person, who under this scenario would be regarded as an enemy.

The spirit, (which is you) must be satisfied, with all offerings, from the self, towards the world, in order to stay healthy and honest. If this would not be the case, then the spirit would be dominated by negative forces of resentment, jealousy and contempt. This would make a person do hideous acts which, over the period of time, would make a person feel guilty. He would regret going against his intuition and would be sorrowful for being astray from the path of righteousness and truth. It must be realized that guilt is a constant companion that never lies, and is only against those that try to ignore its howls, from within!

In order to get rid of the monotonous wrath of guilt, try to revisit the areas where you have been wrong or where you have exploited the situation for your own benefit. Try to undo your evil acts of selfishness, by being generous and by giving back to the society at large, with the generosity of your love and kindness.

*The Thumb Demon, (inner negative energy, which uses you to mess up your own blessings, and also alters temptations of the mind), becomes the primary enemy against a human. I will reveal the temptations of such demon and its helpers, which suck the positivity and in-turn the hope of life from all the humans, to a degree that there is no life left in him. To get rid of these demons is the "best way to get anything in life"

"The Laws of the Physical Dowel"

This Dowel stands on the bottom end of all the other Dowels; however, it is equally important since it expresses the combined force of the rest of the Dowels through physical actions and reactions (both verbal and non-verbal). For this Dowel to be understood, uphold the physics and the value of the verbal assets of your actions.

As part of the discussion on physical dowels, I would like to mention that 'tongue' is just as physical a human asset, as the sensation of touch. Each Dowel, along with the physical dowel, brings forth an effort, which reveals the intention and energy associated with it. So, keep a closer check on your words and your actions. You actions dictate your behaviour and your behaviour is a reflection of the type of spirit you have.

Physical products of each dowel, without using the external body parts, are listed below;

The Physical output of Mind: It is the use of the mind to move all parts of the body.

The Physical output of Emotions: The expressions of feelings of a human being, which do not require any physical act, are emotions. The body language, the physical gestures and the usage of the words are some of the examples of physical outputs of emotions.

The Physical output of Spirit: The underlying intuitions, guilt, and spiritual workings, in physical form, connecting the physical, and spiritual self are the physical outputs of spirit.

Spiritual connection Tunnel: The spiritual connection tries to remind the human beings that whatsoever is given to them by nature is to be honestly retuned to it by threefold. Whatever is intended by nature has a reason behind it and these reasons are dictated by our actions and choices.

The right proportions of the outputs of mind, emotions and spirit would help you to make right decisions. Use your strengths to fulfil the tests of Nature. To know whether you are being tested by Nature, you must observe, recognize, and acknowledge, the functions and actions of nature. Nature is an unflinching teacher and to learn from in, you must utilize all your senses.

Refer to pint 3&4 of section sacred numbers to complete lesson on this.

"SACRED NUMBERS"

As a human, you must have encountered a number of troublesome and challenging situations, throughout your lives. Some of these problems may have been so tough, that for a time being, you must have felt that you have reached a dead-end. To solve such problems, you must stay hopeful and look for a simpler method or a way to approach these problems. Once you have devised a successful technique to help you approach a problem, use the learning from this practice to solve all your future difficult situations. You would realize that the technique that has worked the first time to solve a problem would always be handy and can be applied to every troublesome situation, only with minor changes. You must find an all natural way upon making your own methods fit the problem, as one's own outstanding solution. You are to practice this continuously, unless it becomes a habit and creates a rhythm of harmony in your lives. You are to soon master this and then pass it on to others, so that you can be a light in the darkness for the people who are less fortunate or are swarmed by problems.

Sacred numbers are not ordinary numbers, as perceived by a common human mind, but they are symbols associated with methods to solve a difficult problem. These symbols act as solutions in situations of difficulty and can be applicable to a number of related problems. A number would be assigned to a method devising solution to a problem, just to distinguish it from all other solution methods. The number would denote the uniqueness of the solution method. Reutilizing values that had been found within a method and using the key-learning points from that situation to other situations, is known as "Tooling". You may hear the word tooling throughout this book, but reading through the entire text, you would eventually start to understand the real purpose of the tooling method in your lives.

Right now I am about to present a small list of 'sacred numbers', which will soon help you to find, and create solutions, no matter how bad the problem may seem to be. Majority of these numbers are for you to use, individually, or to pass on the learning from this book to your friends, who would find their presence useful in their lives. Do your part as an individual, and as part of your society, (may it be local or worldwide.) The other numbers, you will see in this list is for you all to get together and make these things happen for the world.

The list of sacred numbers has been produced below;

Energy Hemming- Used to bring in improvements in the self or others

Nature's Grand Odom- This can be used by everyone. Grand Odom signifies that we are a part of larger creation of God and therefore we must live in nature cohesively and should welcome any other God's creation to be a part of our Grand Odom, if they are willing to join in.

Stairway towards Success- It is also used for self-improvement and to suggest improvements in others.

Shift Book- Used to better the self and others.

Observing problems so that the problem would reveal a solution to you- Used to better the self and others.

Making that what you already have, even better, and futuristic, by also using the sacred number 8 called "tooling". It is for you to improve the present, by taking that what you have, and making it better by adding add-ons and ideas, from many other projects, of the Earth. You are to grow and help grow by adding on, and giving the feel of a more futuristic twist, to life.

Defeating the Greys- for all humans to use together by working with a prior problem, now being able to be used as a method of its own, in various situations. This is to be used to better the self and others.

Tooling- As discussed earlier, tooling would use the learning from prior problematic situations, to solve the new problems on hand. This is to be used to better the self and others.

The Olarah Control-(Recognizing the genuineness, along with the errors in self, as well as in others) Also it is for you to recognize the problem, or any problem that varies, in your own scenario, using your own intuitions, so that such a problem could reveal to you a solution, sooner. Using the energy coming off of the problem, that bothers you, as a fuel of creativity; Using the common sense to help create a solution type possibility, that could work out, and become the dominate solution. On the other hand one must become well aware of consequences, and blessings that are the results of one's own actions. The greater your awareness would be, the better the results will be for you. This sacred number can also be used to improve yourself and your fellow humans.

0- This sacred number is used foe ideal situations, in which the things turn out to be the way, we want them to be.

I would now be explaining scared numbers 1, 2, 3, 4, 6, 7 and 9 in greater detail. While for the other sacred numbers, like sacred number 5 (which is quite simple and self-explanatory), it does not require further elaboration. The sacred number 8, on the other hand, would be discussed in further detail, during the course of this book.

{{Sacred Number 1:"Energy Hems"}}

Energetic Hems are the ultimate tool for mastering mental, emotional, spiritual and physical control on all other people. If you were to master this tool, you would ultimately have greater influence on people. The recognition of the real situations of life is the first step to bring in improvements in life. The art of hemming energy be of a magnetic pull, which draws certain types of attention towards you, let it be that of a blessing, or a down fall. It all depends on one's own understanding of the concepts, being based on hemming energy.

The art of hemming energy would be discussed in greater detail throughout this book, so that you can have a detailed insight into the workings of this energy. Being the personality that you are, your own personality could also become used as that of a working charm, for others to see things your way, if only known by you, in your own natural way, upon how to hem energy. Your personality is the projection of you, in the eyes of others and helps you to gather feedback from them. Your personal traits dictate the behaviour of others towards you. If you would have a pleasing personality, people are more likely to connect to you and are more likely to leave a positive feedback for you.

Manipulation is a strong word, and it is used in varying ways by the masses in general. The art of hemming energy, parallels with manipulation(s), but the difference is that with hemming energy the art is being worked out by nature, using things around you as tools; to improve one's self, and to improve situations alike. With hemming energy you are to manipulate situations, using your own personality as tool, towards fixing up the mind and energies, of others. This is for your subjects to perform acts desired by you, or to see things your way, by you saying things, and doing things that you know they would love to hear and/or see on the first hand.

You must observe both, the positivity and negativity of your subject in question, to gain proper information about them. You are not to violate the will of others, using manipulations, of any kind, however only having to protect the self from such a manipulation by those type violators. You must think upon a winning strategy towards getting all of what you want, or need, in all the best of ways, being seen as fit for the journey. This art is to be used towards all others in an honest and trustworthy manner, because if not then the results would probably not look good, because of the natural energies involved with it. Those bad intentions would probably be the reason for the same type of come back, especially if you have bad intentions towards someone else.

You must learn to know how to handle your subjects, from personality observances, that in order to use energy hemming properly, you must learn other people's personalities, just to have something to work with. With this you could also help others further their own goals, do to hard facts that you had now found out about them; helping them to overlook all blocks in their lives. Energy hemming is to also to be used to protect one's own self from negative sorcerers; that all people. It must be realized that not all the people would have good intentions towards you and this would be discussed in great detail in the next section of the book. The act of giving a helping hand, while manoeuvring for the self to succeed is mostly valued by the universe, and should also be valued by you.

Being the owner of your own choices, you are being held accountable by the nature as it sends different types of tests your way. These tests can rightly be regarded as the reactions to your actions, let them be good or bad. You must also comprehend that your Energetic hems have the abiity to bring about change in you are they are dictated by your intentions. It is up to you to understand the impact of your actions on your daily life. You must muster the courage to critically analyze your surrounding situations, fearlessly point out your flaws and avoid similar mistakes in future. You can have full control over your body, its actions and in turn your situation, if you let positive energy be the guide of you and embrace it with all your heart and soul.

The following terms are essential for you to understand, it order to comprehend this lesson in further detail.

Hemmer is someone who can perform the act of humming i.e., a human being

Hemming is the act of using the self in ways to charm others into your own plans i.e. from getting to know how a particular person makes choices, how often do they make choices and what is their most frequent action in face of crisis. It is also important to know the consequences of your action and to make attempts in understanding the context of others.

"A good enough hemmer could weave around obstacles; pluck them out of the way, and path."

"You must figure out the way things work and then figure out a way to work with them, in order to succeed"

This information may be indecipherable for you, as for now, but eventually when you have understood the logic behind tooling, you would eventually be able to decipher the meaning behind these words. Learning how to control the consequences of your actions, or as synonymously said the works of nature is the real objective of this lesson. Manipulation of the situation, in the right and positive ways would ultimately make you the master of self over the years to come. You would become the master of your spirit and in turn would be the God of your fate.

The greatest of energy masters are the ones, who deviously control their own personality in a natural way. Once again, that the sheer master knows how to turn his or her personality into a tool, which will bring about chances out of no chance, love out of no love, and hope out of no hope at all. The only experience needed, that they truly have, by nature, is called "Energy Hemming". I call it this, so that they could recognize this ability with a proper name and an image. Separating such values, away from those intentions that are of deceitful manipulations, and that this be the difference between the two of them. Knowing what to say, how to say it, what to do, and how to do it, in a manner that would be enchanting to the target (as an onlooker) which would also bring back awesome results, if done correctly, by the hemmer. This type of wisdom would only be for the use of righteous acts, and for the purpose of granting the rights to the rightful. That this be of the master, create a new habit and become a new person altogether for the welfare of the mankind.

The more you recognize, and realize, the more critical you will become in the observance of things. This will then increase your ability to focus on the minute details of everything. You would be able to control your own hem work, you would be able to redefine physical situations in a way that would suit you and would then have a stringer control over the situations around you. Energetic hems makes up the fields of nature, as nature would do many of its own workings alone. Therefore, nature is being filled with all kinds of reasons for being.

"The Energetic Tower Of Positive Power"

PLACE PICTURE OF PYRAMID RIGHT HERE, WITH 4 layers. Bottom layer is Layer #1.AND THIS IS PICTURE # 1

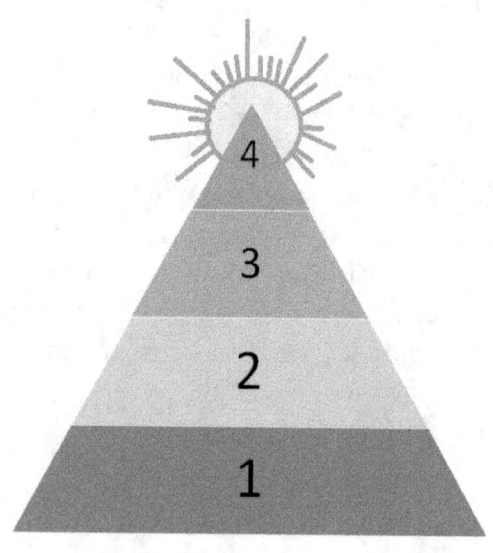

Bottom Level - You all must have a certain type of passion, a desire for success and a future destiny in mind. The destiny may desire a successful future or the hope to be honourable in this world or the worlds to come.

2nd Level - You must plan ahead of time. If needed, I recommend, that you must use the "Stairway towards Success" method. This method is discussed in detail under the heading of the title called "*Methods*". These methods would not only help you to see the intensity of your goals, but it would help you to devise ways through which you can reach the top by fulfilling your goals. "You must strive to be, in order for you to become".

3rd Level - Helping others to find a solution to their problems, is the third step in the energetic tower of positive power. You must be a giving soul with an ability to love and cherish others and to respect them and their opinions. You can only expect to be respected back if you give it to others. The nature follows a viciously reflective cycle of conduct. If you give away love and care, you would get back the same.

4th Level - Positivity should become a habit which would become an inseparable part of your personality. The righteous acts must be practiced so often that they become your nature over the period of time.

In order for you to become a master hemmer, you must master the art of observation and surveillance. It is then that you would have a better understanding of this tool, being from one's own natural experience, to learn from. The key to all hems alike, let it be mental, physical, spiritual, or emotional, and would be referred to as "s*ensing*". That you must sense out the truth, possibilities, lies and all of the needed information, out of that situation, or situations that varies, in order to gain some type of tool to work with. This would help you to recognize the problem and to create a context that would be beneficial for you in the longer run.

THE GRAPH BELOW DEFINES YOU, AS THE HEMMER, AND I WILL GIVE DEFINITION ON AS TO HOW TO HANDLE THE PEOPLE THAT SURROUND YOUR EVERYDAY LIFE. REFER TO THE FIGURE FOR DETAILS.

THIS IS PICTURE #2

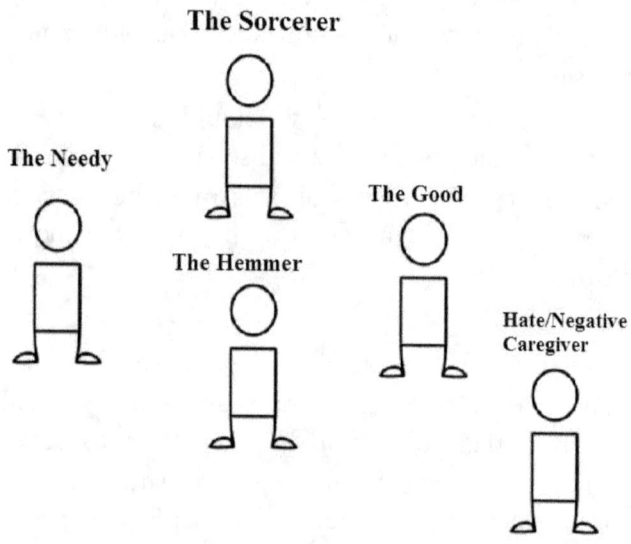

As a hemmer you must be very observant and you must learn how to do the right thing at the right time.

You must muster the art of explaining yourself and getting the desired information from others. As a hemmer, you must know what to say when and how to decode situations, in order to understand their meanings and then act accordingly. You must learn about the subject (person or a thing) to know it. You can do this by observing the subject, and allowing it to reveal itself with clues over a period of time.

Interaction gives us something to work with and reveals a lot of information about the subject in question. It decodes the value of the things for a good observer. The art of saying the right thing at the right time, the way to say it and the right choice of words are the greatest tools in convincing others to agree with you. . Therefore the approach towards any other person should be made only for helping hands, good company, survival purposes, and for you to succeed, in any situation, using others as tool.

You must a friendly, open and accepting personality while you are in a personal conduct towards others.

It is vital to be forthcoming especially once the manners of the particular person have been figured out and are good enough to deal with. However, your personal observance towards others, should always remain sharpen and the critical analysis of a person should be the primary focus of the observer. It is for you to hang around just to observe more, with interest, and to make sure whether that person is being genuine enough for you to have a long term relationship with. The best approach from then on is for you to try and keep things cornered. To do so, you must become trustworthy, truthful, loving, helpful, and respectful and create friendly situations, so that it is easier for the person to interact with you. In return, if the act of friendliness is properly executed, the target would begin to trust you, would listen to you and would love you in return. In case they decide to get closer to you, they would provide solution to your problems, if not solve them for you. You must observe both the target's good and bad side, so that you could define the boundaries of your relationship. Creating agreeable and supporting situation with your friends would make others trust you in the long run and eventually, you would have a upper hand in the relationship.

Creating a situational hook can also be used as a tool, towards drawing both truths and lies to the light. A situational hook is created when you use your own wonders and doubts, as target, towards finding out and confirming a certain truth. Say things to eradicate truths and stimulate responses from your friends, ask questions to clear your doubts and confusions and be specific in your conduct with a chosen friend. Mix your own intuitions (wonders) in with real possibilities, about the situation. Focus on the situation and try to be truthful, while accepting only truths as answers.

-*Hemmer interacting with negative caregivers*-

On a much more positive note, negative personalities can be moulded by you if you reveal the love, care and positivity associated with your personality to them. It is for you to employ love, by giving to them a certain type of respect, to start with. It should be the type of respect, you know, would be demanded by them. It is from the observance that you will get more, out of the target, to work with, as tool (knowing what to say, how to say, what to do, and also how to do it.) If not wise enough to know how to do this, then stay out of their way.

Remember my dear class of geniuses, which this approach really means a lot and it is also for you to remember that for the good of all things, one must have a good starting point. You must build a report with your subject in order to change them. The first step for you to change others is to surrender your own ego. Start with care and respect. The physical display of love with words and emotions should be left for a later stage since it would set string grounds for a stronger relationship in future. To most negative care givers, trying to show early claims of love is only a sign of weakness and it is among one of the reasons for as to why one should study the target 1st. so that he or she could know how to approach them, and make way for themselves to give care, and show respect in ways that would influence the target as time being spent, goes by. "Knowing how to use one's own surrender, as a bate tool, towards succeeding" should also be the key to defeat wars, and all other negative energies. Surrender as in giving in to minor suggestions, for the sake of major changes being made for the better.

The greatest key to start with, when dealing with negative care givers be communion (keeping things on a safe honest level, coming from you, as the hemmer) and also be that of loyalty unto them. These things will give them reasons to reside by your side. "Do not judge anyone" is the law; yet try to understand them. In order to understand them, you must evaluate the situation in which a person is operational and them be empathetic to them. It is for you to become a great friend unto them, to try and soften up their hearts from so much negativity, by giving unto them keen enough suggestions, to their own ideas. Master this, with time being spent doing so, and you will then gain that natural feel, of things and control of things being your way. The energy, from within them, as being the target, would magnetically come to the point to where you are now of an interest to them. Once influenced by your ways, they would begin to see things differently, that being helpful, and having good friends isn't a bad idea at all, which would influence them to act, and react in a different way, as time being spent with them, by you, goes by. In the earlier stage of relationship development, "the good feeling" would be the influential seed. Use the softening of their heart and their good feeling as a ground to strengthen relationships with them. Make them realize that you are there for them under all circumstances, where good or bad. Convey to them that "*this good feeling is to be passed all around the entire world, and I am going to help you all do so*".

If you catch the negative care-giver in act of lying or betrayal, you must realize that it is their secret wish for you to keep it undercover. They would not like others to know of their shameful act and would expect you to hide it for them. If you reveal their secret to the world, they would see you as their enemy and would refuse to trust you in future. But if you (as the hemmer) were to forgive them, right then and there, keeping it all in between you and them (if could), or (if have to) ward off all that wishes to point negative fingers at them, it would get back to the negative caregiver that you was taking up for him or her, and this would give you an upper hand on the seeding process. You (as the hemmer) must consol the negative caregiver, by making him realize that you are on his side. You can do this by saying kind things like, it is okay to make mistakes and it is okay o be a part of system that illicit evil in you. You must not pass value judgements and make the caregiver realize that you love him no matter what and that despite everything; you would always stand by his side. This act of acute kindness would place them right into the palm of your hands. You are to continue to show them that you care, and that you can be trusted. If they leave something on, it is for you to turn it off; it is for you to show them that you are worthy to become a great pal. At this moment, you are to give to them a form of trust called "Troll's trust"(in which this type of trust is to make someone feel that they are being trusted, but in reality they are being tested) that this form of trust, could indeed turn into the real deal, if all the righteous choices, is being made by your target (The negative caregiver).

If this tool becomes hard to be applied at certain places, I advise you to not to worry about it, since it is not necessary that every person would relate to you. Those who may not listen to you may be more open and friendly towards another person. The negative caregiver may reject you, but it by no means, signifies your failure as a hemmer, but it only implies that they would connect more properly to some other person. However, in 90% of the cases, if you use your hemming power right, it is more likely that the negative caregiver would listen to you and would like to be associated with you. You have to learn from your experiences, and sharpen up your own skills, during this journey. Therefore, this book is to be applicable worldwide, for all to find their placing, and join hands energetically using the positive motivations.

It must be noted that the message of love and care, that this book cohesively imparts to the mankind is very important. If majority of the world decides to learn from the lessons of this book, they would all soon become positive hammers and while coming in contact with negative caregivers, they would be able to mould them accordingly. If the basics of Olrah Control become mastered by all the humanity, it would drastically increase the level of awareness of all the people around the world. People would try to tell the truth, shun the lies and would try to surround themselves with positive people. They would also caste a positive influence on the liars or the negative caregivers, who would eventually learn from the good conduct of hemmers and would soon, adopt a positive personality. This would influence the liar to become more aware of his or hers flaws in the art of lying, in the end finding out that a method in this book will always reign over any bad intentions or any other flaws of the personality. This book would also devise methods for healing the self and would also suggest ways to accomplish your goals by reaching the top, without any help from any other leader. This book will teach you how to get rid of bad karma, without meditation skills, nor astral travel. Everything in this book is made out in an all natural way, for the human race to become manifested by the number and that this book will influence many circles of people, if they give it a through reading. I would like to reveal the portion of personal experience here, by affirming the fact that I have a very strong relation with nature. It is so strong that I and nature seem to have a perfect bond of cohesion and attraction. By imparting my wisdom to you, I also want be a hemmer and a helper. Make the best of your efforts to use these methods only positively. If you make a negative use of them, they would backfire and the result would soon become visible.

-*The Interaction of Hemmer with the Needy*-

If you are a good person, with a passion towards helping and healing situations, this part would be relatively simpler for you. Helping those in need gives you an ultimate upper hand, but you must make sure that the needy are truly in need, because you do not want your hard work to be wasted. Our objective, from here onwards is to eliminate as much falsehood from the universe as possible, and it would only be doable if we recognize the acts of the negative caregiver, understand the tendency of the false act and that you have the ability to approach it properly. As a hemmer, you must recognize these acts, should know the art of dealing with them and it is important for you to know as to how to reveal them to others. If it is important to disclose their conduct to other people, do it tactfully and with care. Use light and digestible humour to make a point about them and make sure that the negative caregiver gets a hint about the purity of your intentions. As a hemmer, it is your responsibility to identify the roots of the falsehood, reveal them to the people and then try to uproot it from the very depth. The mere exposure of the falsehood would weaken its very foundations and would discourage the beholder of such evil acts to engage in them. Revealing such acts would strengthen the awareness of others around you, as they would pay much more attention to you, out of interest. They would see it as an opportunity to add value to their learning and would develop trust in you.

You need to help out the needy as if it was nothing but the right thing to do. Soon, others would follow your footprints and a natural cycle of help, respect and care would start in the society. Remember, it is important for you to follow the tool of *master motivation*. At this level of motivation, the interest of the others should be the key motivation of the hemmer. As a person dedicated for the welfare of the humanity and must give promising suggestions after analysing the situation in which the negative caregiver is. Once the negative caregiver realizes that you are well-informed about the consequences of his situation, he would eventually let you take the lead. However, in order to make them feel superior and by interacting them at a subliminal level of their psyche, you as the master, must pretend that you are a step under them. In this way they would subconsciously accept your presence as a leader and would let the seed of love that you have planted inside them to flourish.

Let's take a scenario where I am the master and

my target's name is Chris.

Chris wants to be able to do his math work, but have no confidence in him or the drive to complete it as per the schedule. Even though I know how to do the work (and I have the ability to teach him how), I must exercise the art of pretence where I pretend that the mathematical calculations are equally hard for me. I should continue with this act until I stir a drive for learning in little Chris, which in turn would motivate him to do his work more carefully. Chris will then go for what he knows, and soon will get it right. As a teacher, I would pass little hits to Chris and when he gets the question right, I would pretend it was the product of his own hard-work. This would make Chris feel confident and smart and he will be motivated to try even more difficult questions of the same pattern. I being a motivator, would now become a likeable and acceptable entity for little Chris. At this point, I can encourage Chris even more by using uplifting words of praises and motivation and by telling him how smart he was at this, since even I was not able to figure out the right solution. This motivation would make Chris realize that no one is better than other and only hard work and a continuous struggle is the ultimate key to success. My labelling Chris more astute than myself, I have made my target feel good about himself, while subliminally accepting me as a figure of authority.

In trade, one could request help from those he or

she had helped once before. Remember that this is not for any selfish needs, but it is being fit for those needs that are selfless and gallant.

Let's discuss another alternate scenario here. Mr. Walker is a man of great character and is charitable and noble in his manners. He feeds the needy, provides them with shelter and restores their faith in humanity by promising a brighter future where they would grow and flourish. Mr. Walker now asks for a favour from all of them in return. It is important to note here that the audience in Mr. Walker's case are from different nations. He asks his audience to forgive their rivals, to start with. Second, he asks them to reveal their best selves to their enemies, in a way that it would elucidate positive feedback from them. He makes them realize that unnecessary rivalries breed hatred and contempt, which in turn destroys the peace among the nations. He makes them accept the fact that they need a peaceful and nonviolent world, not only for themselves but for their children and grandchildren. Mr. Walker pronounces war as a waste of time, money, efforts and human lives and regards it as the root of all the evils. He advocates the case of a warless world by claiming that the foundation of a peaceful world is in our hands. If we choose make our lives a living hell, it would be a personal choice of self-destruct and failure. In order to have living peace on the planet, first step is very crucial. Mr. Walker investigates from his audience that "whether they want to thrive in a world of peace and serenity where they are equitably fed, sheltered and fairly clothed, without any fear of being attacked by an enemy of the similar breed but a different race?" The answer of passionately asked question was an empathetic "*affirmation*" from his audience.

Mr. Walker then said "Well lets end all tensions, and gain full control of our lives, by being the first to surrender in the face of pointless violence. When we would stop destroying the gifts of nature by setting fire to them, the nature would bless us itself with resources, wisdom and knowledge. Our love would be reciprocated by nature in the form of happiness."

The ultimate aim of this mission would be to foster love, peace, and togetherness all over the entire world. To find out more, on this type of filtration, such values could now be found within this book under the chapter entitled "*Nature's Grand Odom*". I would use my person experience as a part of example under that section of the book. I would, and then introduce my representatives in each part of the world, through my work. They will then give my words to their people, the same way or similar to the way it had been given unto them, which will be of the righteous plans, towards a relief; being prepared for them to become friends and family with rivals(making rivals once rivals). That newer ways of life would soon begin from all of this, by me using the "Angels of The Light" method, which could also be found in this book. These methods would grant relied and peace to all the people of the world.

-Hemmer against Sorcerers-

Most of the times, sorcerers would choose to work up against you without you even knowing it. Life not going well, for you, is just about all you would come to know, about this situation, majority of the time. So we must go for what we know, now, in order for us to get rid of the negative magnetism being placed in our lives, by others, and it is for us to not give them any room. Who do you think that it is, working up against you? Who cares? Let's just defeat the purpose of their intentions by us all not allowing them to exist, any longer in our life. It is for you to see where you are trying to go, using the "Stairway towards Success" method, (found in this book) and it is for you all to place self discipline over all.

Sorcerers usually work through laziness, anger, sleepiness, weaknesses and imaginations that would encourage you to make choices,(designed for you), against your own will, that this be the sorcerer's desire, being fixed up by an energetic source (being chosen) as the influence.

These type of people want you to give up, they really want for you to be out of their way, but as for now all of that will cease to be the case. You now have the choice to allow, or not allow these things to come about, but a good enough self discipline would kill the very intentions of their diabolical plans. Set yourself, your goals and how you are going to accomplish these goals, for the self. It is for you to become dedicated to your plans, step by step, move by move, without procrastinating, without allowing anger to mess up blessings, without getting tardiness to take away your motivation when you are striving to achieve your goals. Stop leaving your work for the later date since this would mess up your plan and would disrupt your daily routine. Become dedicated to your goals without allowing temptations to influence you to dismiss your plans. Temptations like these are usually being granted by friends, family, and sometimes enemies; that this is usually done by them unconsciously and without often without any bad intention. It is up-to you to be determined and self-reliant and say no to them at the right time. Limit and monitor your imagination and do not let pointless thoughts to sway your mind. Be the master of your mind and concentrate on your goals so that you can get desired results by the end of the completion of your task.

It is important for you to learn to be happy under all circumstances and to become self-disciplined. It is for you to become strong and resist these feelings and take a strong stand against laziness. By being strong and standing up against all the negative energies, sorcerers and negative caregivers; you are eliminating all of your weaknesses and are moving a step closer towards your goals. Watch out for the root causes of the negative energy; once you have identified those sources, stay away from them and stay focused on your goals, which ultimately would grant you internal satisfaction and happiness. You get a limited amount of pleasure by engaging in useless activities, however, the happiness you would get from achieving your goals would be eternal and life-long.

The above discussion is trying to help you to block those thoughts which urge you to stay away from your goals by saying; "Hey, let's do this work late and focus on something else for the time being." Defeat all the negative energies that are trying to overpower your common sense by staying happy, motivated and focused on your goals. Do not worry about anyone who tries to come in your path o attaining your goals, instead summon up all your courage and energies and direct all your attention towards your life objectives.

The first step on the path of ultimate success is to, first of all, identify the goals and plans. "A *tool to mould the inner-self*" method, discussed under the section "*The stairway towards success*", would help you identify the real purpose of your life. These methods would prepare you well for your future journey. Success in attainment of life goals would only be possible if you would strive tirelessly, defeat the hurdles of your path and find an approachable method to solve all your problems. Devise a step-by-step plan to attain your goals and use your energies as a hemmer to become victorious in your life.

{{Sacred Number 2:"Nature's Grand Odom"}}

The list discusses the rationale behind human nature and comments over the nature instincts of man that are most valued in this universe.

Charity- The complimentary act of one form energy, facilitating another form, in need, through the physical form, of human's reality.

Teaching the art of righteousness- Under this phenomenon, human beings take pleasure in teaching the right thing to their fellow humans. The helper or the hemmer would impart this knowledge in his own natural and kind manner. The chosen targets would be influenced by the wisdom of the hemmer and would eventually start to get closer to him. Learning from the hemmer, the target would eventually become a hemmer himself and would pass on your knowledge to the entire world. This would start a positive cycle of helping human beings and righteousness would take over the planet. It is important for every one of you to pass on your knowledge to your family and friends to be a source of ultimate change in this world. Be dedicated from your heart with whatsoever you do and passionately connect with the people and influence them with your knowledge. This way you would get internal satisfaction and would also be a source of ultimate happiness for your fellow human beings.

Be committed- Commitment, dedication and love shows from the eyes. When you would be resolute to spread the light of truth and righteousness throughout the world, it would be reflected by your eyes.

These acts of kindness and dedication would spread the message of compassion in the world, would take away negative tensions from the lives of people and peace and serenity would prevail. People would be more relaxed in mind since they would always believe that eventually everything is going to be alright. This would then start a cleaning process for the universe. Universe would engage in the natural cycle of giving back to the humanity i.e. if we would decide to live with harmony and peace on this planet, the universe would also return us love and affection.

{{Sacred Number 3 & 4:"Stairway towards Success & The Shift Book"}}

The following sets of advices are applicable and valid for people belonging to all spheres of life. Follow the following steps to get a detailed insight into these steps;

1- Get a pen and a tablet

2- On the first page of your list, vertically list down your traits and what you are right now as a person. Now list down your most desired goals at the top so as to signify where you want to be by the end of this exercise. It must be noted that a separate page must be assigned to each goal so as to provide you with sufficient room to ponder over your options. This exercise would allow you to move from one step in life to the next and then eventually, would help you achieve your all goals. Give a specific and unique title to all of your goals and then devise an action plan for them.

3- Next, it is for you to just sit back and think about how you are going to get from where you are now(which is the bottom step), to where you want to be (which is the very last step, drawn at the top.) .

*4- Next, continue to follow the above steps, of *2 and *3, and list your way, to the top, (from step to step), which is where the main goal shall reside, as a destiny.

Make sure that it all makes perfect sense, and that if you would become dedicated to this plan, it will all come to past. Self dedication, and one's own passion, to do so let it be the very drive needed, on this personal journey to the top.

*5- In the end, you would have a document in the form of stairway to the success.

"THE SHIFT BOOK"--- A SIMPLE TOOL FOR REFORMING THE INNER SELF

This method would demonstrate as to how to redirect your life by gaining greater control over yourself, especially if you are driven by your emotions right now.

I advise you to get a note book to work for this method

This method will show you how to rein-birth your own life, for you to have a greater control, over the self;(especially if not completely controlled by you, now)

Get a note book, just for this:

*Write "Mental Dowel" at the top of the page.

*At the top left hand corner, write (Mental Woes)

*Sit back and ponder over all your mental weaknesses. Write them down in descending order of their importance.

Now critically evaluate your woes.

While critically analyzing your woes, I suggest you to come up with the solution of your problems. After you are done, use the similar method for your Dowels.

Apply the solution to your Dowels and Woes and emotionally and spiritually defeat them. Make these changes in self for better future.

If you need help with your Dowels, go through all of your dowels and try to pinpoint the one with which you are having most trouble with. Read more on that Dowel under the enhancement section and also look out for the woes. After you have reviewed all this, make notes in a note pad for reference in future.

Organizing the Mind, Spiritual grasp, emotional web, and Physical terms of ACTS (as if you was helping out a friend, and you was to give them the perfect solution), by masterminding your life, and purpose to be all that you can be "Honestly", and hopefully in righteousness.

The example in this has been listed below:-

(Mental woes): Start all woes with a problem, then ponder over the solution, followed by a relief to the solution, and then the final quote (final demands). After that ask yourself questions, and then answer them. Always remember that most of the time the answer comes from within your own question.

For example; a problem can be "when I am with my friends, I start smoking due to peer-pressure"

A solution to this problem can be "Stop hanging out with the lot that encourages you to smoke, especially when you consider it as a weakness and want to overcome it for your own betterment. Whenever you feel for a pressing need to smoke, just remind yourself that not smoking would be strength and you want to be a strong person".

Another plausible question relating to this solution can be "What should I do when I find myself in a situation like this."

Solution Relief: "List the main people who have greater influence on your behaviour and attitude"

(Relieving to a solution is like telling on all the problems, to the self, for trade, with the inner nature, using influence towards gaining interest, along with the strength, to overcome, such an obstacle, that had been well recognized.)

Final Quote: "Your final quote is the ultimate action you are going to take to stay out of this problem and then make a final decision and live by it".

Final quote example: "So I have realized that Jim, Kerk and Leon are my prime influencers who encourage me to smoke. I am going to stay away from them until I lose complete taste for smoking. I must cut them out for a time-being for my own personal good"

Q&A

What if Jim sees you hanging around, in a different area, and asks you why you haven't been around lately?

*I'm a tell him, and all others that I'm trying not to smoke, so I need to stay away from them, for a while, and laugh it off, in the end."But back on point"---> (that is I would never smoke again).

Exercise this method, and watch how much

control you gain back, and strength you will enhance of each dowel. By finding the problems, labelling them as of what they are, coming up with solutions for them, and live by the final Quote, which is the final solution, demanded by you, for you to live by, as an ultimate changing point, in your lives.

If it is difficult for you to find your woes, just think about the things that you do not like about yourself. Find the underlying dowels under these woes, jot them down on a paper and make a resolution to live by your final quote. This exercise would provide you with a simple solution to fix the problems in your life. The step-by-step procedure would also define a blueprint which you would be able to follow in the case of future problems. The process would help you improve your inner self, which in turn would dictate your outer actions.

If you want to monitor your actions thoroughly, the best way would be to go back to your Dowels and read on them again. Make choices and decisions, led by the information you find on Dowels.

These two powerful methods would assist you to make better decisions, lay down simple plans, create your own agendas and would help you find natural ways to overcome your weaknesses. Here, it must be noted that writing down weaknesses and then devising plans on papers help you to follow them more religiously. Since you have written them down, you think it is your duty to follow them. Writing is acclamation which provides you with motivation to overcome your weaknesses.

{{Sacred Number 6: "The Olarah Control"}}

Your perception about a situation or a person, or the way you have chosen to look at a reality influences the way you operate in nature and sets up the course of your actions. The context you choose to look at the world, determines how you interpret reality. The first step in perceptual translation of a situation is the way you understand it. How well you would manoeuvre through out one's own abilities, of the self, in mixed with the very nature of one's own personality.

Remember class of geniuses that (for you, being the individual that you are) any reality, of any kind, and it's chances, being of life possibilities, goes a bit further, in vision, and in physics, once the mind continues to get beyond the basics, while mastering. Nature is part of everything that you do, (so you must always remember this), but what makes it out to be magical is that once recognized, observed, acknowledged, learned, and then mastered through the powers of knowing; the nature around you would change. If you are positive, it would make life easier for you and would open new avenues of success for you. However, if the nature comes hard on you, you must know how to turn the circumstances in your favour. Define your own reality in a way that would benefit you for years to come.

The following a two important steps to guide you understand a situation better.

First Point of Understanding- Being well aware of values, consequences, possibilities, personalities, and patterns involved in your own set choice making plans, and life; and try to understand the context of the situational factors as well. Acquire full knowledge of the factors that control you in order to play a rational role in times of circumstances.

Second Point of Understanding- once you have figured out the nature of your own dealings, from personal observation and self-studies, try to understand your surroundings and the context in which you are operating. Pay close attention to the way things work around you, as well as those involving you, using their core values, so as to become a master of the self.

Question: **Why should I learn to teach these values to others, if I feel that I myself need to learn them first?**

Answer: You must understand that if you want to gain the trust of a person, you should start it with the mutual values of sharing. Let others know that you want them to do better in life by teaching those good ways to approach difficult situations in life. From this point on, you would begin to realize more and more on how nature corresponds to personal, yet social acts of goodness and would reward you in future.

You must become real about the things that you say, and do; taking life and the values associated with it more seriously. I am a living example of how the seriousness towards life in general and goals in specific can turn difficult situations into your favour. The success, I have got by staying dedicated to my goals, has encouraged me to adopt it as a strategy towards life. As the time passes and you continue with accomplishments, it would become a habit to stay loyal to yourself and your laid down objectives. The faithfulness towards self would lead you on the path of truth and self-awareness. I cannot emphasize more the gravity of importance assigned to accomplishing your goals with dedication and resolution. It is the only way to genuinely achieve success in life. You must also get ready for the observers who would notice you putting in your best into your work. It must be noticed that these onlookers can either be your supporters or your haters. No matter how people treat you, once you have made a resolution, you must stand by it.

***Personality Error**- Once a bad habit becomes dominate in one's life; it also becomes well recognized by others. The onlookers, in specific, would take special notice of all your values, since they are close to you and are always observing you. A personality error occurs, when a person presents a false image of them to others, primarily when they are lying or are trying to cover up a lie.

Take an example of your own personality errors,

for instance. These personality errors can either be known to you, or you may not be aware of their existence. Those around you, also notice your personality errors, 8 out of 10 times depending upon the level of originality you have. The onlooker notices your personality errors either by your actions or by your words. You may also, unintentionally have given out vibes that may have caused the onlooker to notice your display of errors.

It is vital for you to understand that lies to the self, excessive pretence and upholding guilt would eventually change your personality. You would no more be free but would become the slaves of your fake self.

*Personality Genuineness- The more honest you are towards others and also towards your own self, the more you would the more truthful you would become and there would be more positive energy associated with your being. Remember the phrase, "The truth shall set you free", because it is an underlying fact and the truth would indeed free you from the chains of empowering lies. Focus onto the power of truth since my work would help you understand its value. . Actually the truth from within the self sets the self free, by breaking away and staying away from guilt, (being of all kinds) and also well known lies; especially when those type of energies tend to turn one's own innocence, from the inside, into pale negativity.

Pale negativity occurs when one is well-aware of the truth but chooses to lie, in order to live in the situation or to continue with the steadiness of the routine. Living a lie targets your positive energies and makes your inner self pale with guilt and self-hatred. You will find the inner demons taking over your body and eventually your positive energy would be replaced by the negativity of thought and error.

Let's survey in detail the personality errors associated with pale negatives and the genuineness of good natures.

Pale negative: Having dishonest energies and the inner demons which over-empower you can change your personality altogether. Perhaps feeding lies to the self, if not to all others, yet a personality that exercises negative actions only brings down the values, of being well off, and that this be pale negative.

Genuineness of the Personality- The greatest of energies, however, being based on this theory, would provide better health, and is indeed a good health tool needed. Good healthy energies vary, at different times, being based on needs, and also the offering of good natures towards all others. The truth is genuine, so is the light and positivity associated with the virtue of truth.

The truth shall set you free, because it gives off an honest energy, and depending on what the truth is, in all, it shall also work in all levels of genuine needs.

The truth makes you a better person, especially if you are a giver of the truth, and light to all others. Truth is required for progression. It is fuel for a healthy soul and houses positive energy within self. The truth, good actions, helping hands, love, respect, and all that be of honesty be also the tools needed, for good health, Magnetically making changes into the universe, by using actions and the intentions behind those actions, right here on your own planet. This type of positive energy should influence you, on becoming a better person and you should spread the light of your positivity among all of the people.

The things that make you happy must always stay in your life. You must not neglect the values associated with a happy element in your life. The impulse of happiness and the power of truth must be used as a tool to guide you in your future. Dream is an abstract concept and it is up to you to give it a meaningful form. Use the values of truth to guide you to achieve your dreams. Devise ways to stay happy under all circumstances so that your life and in turn your personality can be transformed altogether.

Imaginations and the focus behind it, (being natural), is to be used in your own natural way, throughout the naturalism of interest, and of one's own passion. Venting the body, through the mind (from the mind twining energetically with the heart), drains that energy, down to the solar chakra, in which this created energy would now reach out and touch the universe, (using the spirit) from within one's self.

The last two chakras include the spleen chakra and the root chakra. The spleen chakra equators the top and bottom body, from the belt line feeding to the entire body ,as a whole, the proper balances of self made energy; and also the root chakra which be the one that helps all others bring the entire body into a much more relievable state.

These two above mentioned charkas would actively reveal to the body the requests that have been placed on the spirit and on the universe from the solar charka. These charkas, taken together would provide relied to the entire body and would drain out all negative elements of contamination out from your body. Once your self has been healed by these charkas, you would become a source of light yourself. You would have positive ambiance that would not only make you feel light but would also enlighten the people around you. This method can also be used to cast out negative desires. It is important to know that "energetic drain" is significant to change yourself and become a positive person.

Imaginations = Crown chakra

Direct Focus= Brow chakra

Shifting into a phase during meditation, day dreaming, or controlling one's own breathing for comfort, is being agreed upon and energetically shifted by the swallows of the throat= Throat chakra

The burst of all emotions, and 50% of intuitions, needed for all areas= Heart chakra

The inner self tunnel to the universe upon any request= Solar chakra

Relief, other 50% of intuitions= Spleen chakra.

Hormones, the very energy that charges all energetic abilities, being based upon reality, known or unknown= Root chakra

Here, I have an important question for you. How do you feel in general on regular basis? Before you make an attempt to answer this question, let me share my personal experience with you. I am a person of truth, crystal and clear. Lies, pretence and deceitfulness are neither parts of my character, nor the parts of my nature. Therefore, I am delightful to admit the fact that I feel great on regular basis. I am free of all kind of negativities and my days are guiltless. I believe I am a kind of personality I always wanted to be and there I feel good about myself. Here is a little lesson for you from my personal experience. Make attempts to stand by the truth alone; do not express your opinions about things unless you are sure that they are facts. Love your fellow beings and when you make a joke, make sure that it is not mean and is easily digestible by the other person. I abide by these small rules and therefore, my relatives quote me as a 'lovable' person. I am a genuine person who always expresses the truest of his emotions. I offer best of my regards to my friends and all the fellow human beings. I believe that I have considerably achieved what I wanted to be, however, I have adopted a habit of learning from the truest of all human beings if I ever come across them.

It would like to affirm that onlookers love to see me coming. They connect with me at a personal level and see me as a kind influence on their lives. Since they love my personality, they are more likely to listen to me if I try to guide them on the path of righteousness. I always treated truth as my ultimate master and I want you to realize that my love for my readers is eternal. Therefore, I have put in genuine efforts into this book and its publications so that i can help the humanity to get their life on the right track.

Setting the world free from the lie of Science:

*The truth- Remember that the truth shall always set us free, if it upholds us in righteous ways and meaningful manners. Science, on the other hand, would work best only when what has been learned through research would be truthfully passed to the future generations for learning. The lies or the lack of display of proven facts have held the humanity back. Modern day scientist wouldn't have to do past work, all over again, seeking to find truths, so that they could further the interest, that they have upon building a brighter future, for us all. Possessive scientists are the truth of the time. They lie to their peers and to the world of science because of their selfish desires. They want to complete the experiment that they have started themselves and since they want fame, they do not surface their work before it has reached perfection. They fear that their success with the research would be copied by someone else, who in turn, would steal their spotlight of fame. It is true that some of the theories of the scientists have been copied by other selfish peers of them, who failed to realize that it was an immoral act and would push them towards spiritual decline of pale negativity.

Science could be a great tool towards helping us grow into an intellectual world, full of interest. All we have to do now is encourage those of today, to stay honest, for those that would come tomorrow, all for the sake of no more delays. We now encourage our young scientists, and young people of today to become more of an integrated thinker, using integrated thoughts as their interest to criticize their own idols in those fields they are of. That this act alone would begin the bone picking method, or shall I say that it would also reveal the truth away from lies, if any. The truth about science is that it isn't all the way genuine, all dressed up, as lies and truths combined, called science.

Science is good, as long as it comes with hard given facts, being that the truth be the honest truth, and that it could also be proven. All lies need to be separated from all truths, yet gotten rid of upon many requests to the entire world. Until the truth is revealed, we could not move on honestly, without time passing us by, in those scientific fields, and many other fields that had been locked, do to false info.

Scientific Lies

When the scientific lies are told to the world, the world and its future is being held back in several ways. First of all, the lies keep people in the state of constant emotional turmoil. Some fear that the world would end soon and the worst would come their way; whereas, others are humiliated when they spend their lives teaching those scientific facts which are later proven to be wrong on the bases of scientific research that was conducted years before, but has surfaced only recently. Scientists that lie, or hold back truth, and want to be the only in their field would somehow lock their work, by giving the somewhat honest work with an added twist, to keep you amused ;(placing the ball under one of three cups method). Since most of the scientific facts are kept under the table for a longer period of time, there is no way that you can challenge the validity of the research or can question its authenticity, especially if you are a non-science person. Therefore, the source of scientific knowledge could not be as guiding as the torch being passed to the next runner; however, these theories to make sense for a specific period of time since they are the only ones of their 'kind' for a small period of time. The theories which live only for short period of time grant small period of fame to the scientists who have invented them. It is true that some of them have extensive works which they are reluctant to reveal, but since human is immortal, these facts eventually start to surface with their deaths. People with selfish motives like these scientists must acknowledge the fact that truth is eternal and therefore would be revealed eventually.

Example #1

If preparing a sauce requires only ketchup and spices, these types of scientists would claim that their sauce ingredient is tomato paste, spices, corn syrup, and other added stuff. They would misstate the ingredients in order to invite attention towards themselves and to assign important to their work.

Example #2

Religious scientific fraud- Providing specific year dates for dooms day is the biggest fraud played by scientists or the religious scholars. This has led to the manipulation of the masses. Many were forced to leave their homes; the rest sold their properties and gave money for charity in order to prepare them for the last day. This happened several times and the most popular instances are that of 1999 and 2012. It was predicted that the Sun would burn the earth, a comet would hit water creating fierce waves and it was also predicted that natural disasters would hit the world hard. These predications proved to be devastated for people since they did not only lose their wealth but also their mental peace.

{{Sacred Number 7: "Defeating the Greys"}}

My dear class of geniuses, I would like you to know that life is not about defeating your rivals. In order to win them over, you must learn to overcome the intentions that tend to be threatening, especially towards the entire world. Now just because the Greys have some sort of super technology, and threatening skills, doesn't mean that he human race needs to look at them as being too powerful (especially to handle), because they are not that powerful. They also have agendas, like all other beings, but the human race, however, needs to try and help one another to save the entire planet. The experience I am going to share with you would provide you upper hand in exploitative situations, especially when you have to deal with Greys. I would explain the objectives and interests of Greys in a simple way to you. For you, the approach would never be to approach a grey alien. It is for you to stay out of their way, and to start defeating them, by finding out ways that would defeat their purpose, of using the human's race to kill off its own kind, (being the entire human race) polluting resources of the world, and feeding garbage to the human race, such as manmade food.

You must know that there is a better way to counter this problem, even though it defeats all diabolical purposes. It would help you to build a defence against them. The defence would protect you against any kind of manipulation from them. Using their power of manoeuvring, they can help you to look at the world in a certain way. They would provide a direction to your thoughts; also once they have infected your brain, they would use you against others. Once your brain has started working on the negative frequency instilled in you by them, you would always have fear or future and you would spend your life staying anxious. The fear would influence your decision making skills and you would never know how to solve a specific problem. Other than that you must find a way to calm them down, by finding a way, and making peace that should last forever, yet harm none. I do not hold any negative emotions for extraterrestrials, but I do not stand beside diabolical plans of any species (alien, nor human). I would provide you with ways to defeat their purposes without having to go to war with them. The best way to end Grey's physical threats for the world to come is for you to find and make some kind of bond with them that takes the risk off of the human race, and also the entire world. Along with this I shall give to you some sort of defensive type method, to be used as tool, to help fight off cruel intentions being directed, or as planned to become directed our way.

"About the Greys">"Rumor vs. remedy"
It is said that Greys do not have emotions and have little or

no regard of human life. Also, they are surprised of the virtue of trust that belongs solely to humans.

Teaching them emotions is not easy; however, humans can make an attempt to engage with them in conversation through some medium. One must show them by leading them to each primary emotion, as an example, by using the reality of things, for such a reality to become felt, by the greys, called emotions. They are not human, so they tend to see things differently. The key to this is for you to get them to see things from a human's perspective, by first, getting them to agree. Helping them to find the emotion called "happiness", you must get them to reveal their favourite things to do, and what they wish to become able to do, for the reality of happiness.

Find out a way to reach common grounds with them, using a method that harms no one. Let them know that this list of things, that they do as a hobby, and those things written on the list that they want to accomplish, triggers their very own emotion of happiness, just like certain things that triggers the human being towards being happy.

Dear fellow humans, I have a very important question for you all concerning the circumstances on hand. What method would you adopt to defeat the most intellectual, the powerful and most threatening people or 'things' from another place? It is evident that only a fool would make attempts to defeat a powerful creature like them. It is impossible to defeat them with power or words. Well, even if those supernatural things fail to come in communication contact with the humans, there are other subtle powers associated with humans that have not come to their attention up till now. It is true that the world and hence the universe as a whole is full of surprises, but humans must make attempts to look for a tool that they can use to interact with all extraterrestrial beings. Regardless of the fact that they are almighty, invincible beings, they must have some motives and agendas under which they have taken over our world. What you, as a human can do is to bargain with them by giving them an equally important reason to not to attack the Earth. Your reason just has to be great enough, to them. Make use of the scared numbers given in this book to set the grounds for interaction with these beings. I advise you to use energy hems, primarily, Olrah control, to find out what tempts the Greys, get advice from others that already know more about the subject, would be a good source to acknowledge for the self as well. Knowing what to do, what to say and how to act, (to survive); to get what you want, and need; may it be a specific person place or thing that you would have to go through in order to obtain such values. In this specific case, your art would be to defuse the Greys, get to know them and figure out ways that would encourage them to surrender. Come in the perfect harmony with the world and try to figure out the ways that would make Greys a friend for our world, not its enemy. Plotting plans against the Greys and denying their existence would not help humanity in large, neither would it nullify the probability of their existence. So, there is a vital need to figure out a middle ground that would make both the parties happy. "*Why worry about the upcoming realities when you have perfect solutions for them and can solve it with greater delight and expertise*"

2. *They are being claimed to feed off of human and animal vital fluids, rubbing a liquid formula onto their bodies which is being absorbed through their skin.*

It comes without saying that we need to find a solution to this grave problem. What can be an alternate to the fluids of humans? What can substitute the need for to feed on humans? Which activity can replace the need to feed on human blood? It is true that every human being and his life are important for him and his family. However, the blood and body fluids of the dead human beings is either used for science experimentation, with their consent or it has no use at all. The body fluids of dead humans can serve as a source of food for Greys. However, it must be noted that it should not be the rule but is only a suggestion, which can be carried out only if the families of the dead approve of it. The presence of the Grey can serve as a method to control terrorism in the world in the way that the authorities can threaten the wrong-doers that their fluids would be fed to the dead in case they do not leave their foul acts. Please do not be terrorized by this, seemingly harsh suggestion, since it is only meant as a joke. If push comes to shove, the vital fluids of the freshly dead, that have not donated blood, should be eligible for the donation of vital fluids to the Greys. If have to do so, make mention to the entire world that we support, and honour those citizens of the entire world, that donates their blood to the needy, so that those who do not donate their blood could benefit the humanity later by donating their fluids for the Greys.

It would be like waiting to find every roach in the house, but to do so you must place the food out on your own, instead of allowing them to scramble all over, looking for crumbs. This away would bring them all at your plate, at your chosen time. Think about that.

3. *They also suck the energy of the soul, and many believe that the Greys are in search of soul- partners. They want to steal the soul matrix of humans.*

*We have humans here on Earth that knows how to create souls, and they are called Jinn masters. We could hire them to create souls for the Greys, to experiment and to feed off of as well. Make sure that the souls are full of emotions that are positive.

4. *They are technologically advanced than humans and therefore have the ability to insert memory patterns and consciousness, in clones, in any pattern or in any manner. They are experts in manipulating humans and they have the ability*

to pick out your emotions, thoughts and experiences. They are said to be masters of mind control, and mental implantation techniques.

It is true that they have assumedly sophisticated technology than humans but they cannot implant things in you, if they are unable to make you their prisoners. However another way for them to get you to become manipulated is through earth events, that would trigger you to think in a direction desired by the Greys themselves, as they would use manipulated humans as tool. Look at the intentions of the Greys, and then look at the similarities of situations, of the world. Notice the popular behaviours of the human race, the pollution on the Earth and the diversifying human race. Easily manipulated human beings are those whose egos can be easily challenged and who engage in war like behaviours to take over the world. They are able to have full control over people with negative energy and use them as tools to destroy the world. However, I am fixing to show you how to ward them away from your physical body, how to stay away from becoming manipulated by them, as they would use the world around you to get to you, by allowing many unpleasant influences to widespread, from manipulated leaders (such as local, non-government, government and global manipulation to control your friends, family, and enemies through music, Television, and world news). The world around you would eventually become nothing but a stage they have set for you to play upon.

Considering all the above facts, it is important for you to keep a close check on the amount of liberty you have granted to your leaders. Have a close check on the progression of the events around you, so as to avoid the influence of Greys upon you. You do not want to be the puppets in the hands of the Greys, so be aware of all your surroundings. It is important to monitor all of your actions and the events of daily conduct. It is a general observation that women, nowadays, are treated as sex objects and men are taken as nothing but money-making machines. This is happening since you all are influenced by the power of negative energies which would soon take over your entire being and would in-turn govern the world around you. Fear, usually takes hostage of the good hearts of the world, as they would scream out "Why?" without having a good reply back.

"Fighting off the Greys"> As already discussed, Greys are manipulative beings which use humans, to wage war against fellow humans. They spread evils and implants hatred in the hearts of humans. They aggravate and spread the vices of racism, sexism and chauvinism. They want humans to believe that they themselves are the reason for all the chaos that is happening around them and do not want them to be aware of their existence. Their power stems from their ability to lies they use to manipulate humans. They are very smart. They have an objective, and it doesn't look good at all. However I will show you how to handle them the exact opposite way of being handled by them. They want to play crazy, so we are going to play crazy. They want to destroy Earth using manoeuvred beings, instead what we can do is to influence them and make them our friends so that the greatest threat to human beings can be eliminated. The methods I have laid down are meant to help and heal and not for destruction and devastation, therefore, I want you all to pay close attention to my words.

1. Uproot the vices from the society so that the Greys cannot breed on them. Adopt love as an eternal strategy towards each other and try to tie a knot with your enemies and rivals. . You all must start the process of coming together, for this will be the 1st. major blow, yet you are to only act as if they do not exist, and live your life, but keep them in mind for protection. Keep listening and I'm a give you more on this.

There are many diabolical people out to influence many others towards separation, greed, and all other negative activities.

The Greys plant the seed, and as it grows you will never seem to place your finger on the real reason behind it all, but yet you will always be able to look back to find another humanistic reason for everything. They are well hid and they are very smart. They got the world going for now, and the greatest trick is for you to believe that they do not exist, because they need for you to believe that, which will leave you vulnerable to their presence if wanted to visit you, and vulnerable to their fears being cast out by the nature of people. Yeah, you see now you have ordinary people going with the agenda and not knowing it, but had became influenced by their leaders(governmental, and nongovernmental, right along with leading friend family and enemies that have some sort of control over you) So this poison is minor and major. So remember what I said for you to do by the "Majority", and now let's continue.

Using "Nature's Grand Odom" would be great, as to help in this case. Now look back at the Grey's agenda(s), (if not known then look them up, because it can be found within this book, right in this subject, about the Greys, for simplest term, or you could just look the Greys up by searching for hardcore researchers of the scientific world, the choice is yours. I just recommend that if you decide to go with researchers, on your own, make sure you keep the sacred numbers handy, at all times; especially this one called "The Olarah Control" that could be found in this book, and for all that are interested, I wish for you all to pay a much more closer attention to the Greys, and also leaders of this world;) the reality around you (being the entire world) would then make more sense to you, dealing with minor and major problems of the Earth, and it's atmosphere.

Remember, it is vital for you to pay close attention to all of my words. Follow the method that was taught under sacred number 9. Dear class of geniuses, make attempts to recognize the problem. The problem should be crystal clear so that attempts can be made to map out ideas for solution. In order to achieve success, you must start the process with yourself. Use yourself as an object, which is kind and sophisticated to his subjects. All it takes is your own natural powers of common sense, creativity, and reality seeking, for possibilities, truths, and also lies, for strength and knowledge to be known; you will not only become brighter, but you will also become a master of awareness. This will grant you more mental power and in turn would give you mental protection against the intervention of Greys. You would become more aware about the evils of your surroundings and would eventually have full control on the daily circumstances. You will learn more about the need to stay righteous and would soon get to see the advantages associated with the honourable life. Purity of thought and action is conspicuously needed to ward off evil, specifically the Greys. If you adopt the path of truth, the Greys would not be able to mentally abduct you, nor would they be able to manipulate your physical actions. Needless to say those extraterrestrials breed on negativity of thoughts and actions and use the demons of humans against them. By keeping yourself pure and straight also carries energy of positivity that would ward them off. This would not only keep a human on right path, but would protect him from the unforeseen circumstance of the future and would keep him away from guilt and remorse. The knowledge I am going to give you would not only ward off the Greys, but it will help you ward off their evil intentions as well.

In order to ward of the Greys, you must understand that the world of reality and contemplation is of dire importance for you. You must try your level best to save yourself from the misguided facts presented by media. Moreover, you should not get influenced by poetry or media in the time being. You must dedicate your utmost attention to deviate all kinds of evil away from your life, which can only be done by using scared number 9 i.e. "The stairway towards success". This sacred number would teach you the importance of focus in your life and would help you to stay concentrated and resolute. It will save you from the influence of negative elements in your environment. You can get influenced by a hasty habit which makes you lazy, or the hatred may influence you to take strenuous decisions in life. You may be influenced by the dreamy or romantic poetry written by the poets or by the songs of the song-wrights. Moreover, the news on the media may influence you to hate the people of another nation. The extreme form of influence can be when you stop loving and adopt conspiracy and hated as the ultimate approach towards life. It is true that there are several types of elements that influence us each day, but is up to us to ward them off, so as to be content in our lives.

In order to protect yourself from the paranoia of media, entertainment and from the mild wrath of poets, you must have some solid goals and you should follow those goals with passion and love. A dream must be translated into reality of words and actions. Materializing a dream to the world of reality is the most challenging task but a resolute man can do it without any difficulty or without any fear. My dear genuineness, I would advise you to give your heart and soul to your dream. This can be done by following my laid down 'stairway towards successes. I would like you to know that television and music are not the sources of distraction for those who have full control over themselves and are not easily distracted by hype or by propaganda. Negativity is the main thread in all of the Greys agendas towards the human race, (using the race against one another) allowing all tensions to grow with time, and multiply.

Make sure that your goals, using "Stairway towards Success" do not have any diabolical suggestions to go by. Becoming a master of self with this book and even then playing a negative role in society would be like facilitating the actions of the Greys. Therefore, make a resolution and stand by it. Be a source of help and light for others. Let go of negativities and use the sacred method "The shift book" to help yourself, as well as, to help others. In this way, you would not only become a source of positive influence on others, but soon the positive energy would engulf you.

My book is an attempt to spread righteousness and truth in the world. This work would spill the seeds of goodness, which in turn would fertilize the entire universe. I hope that the radiations of positivity would affect one person and the next and eventually the world would be peaceful place for everyone.

{{Sacred Number 9:"Counting your Blessings"}}

Leroy Walker now intends to provide a lecture on numerology to the entire world. He has made an attempt to deliver this lecture since he hopes that everyone would get assistance from it.

This is the next level of control, over one's own blessings. The very act, of control, and authority in nature, is now being paralleled, with the sense of numbers, as numbers, and actions both adds up, to the perfect sense, as the both of them together, helps keep actions organized, with a good understanding, on how an individual can take this chart and also indulge in many other ways, as well.

"The Indulging Numerological Pattern"

0= Cipher

1= Knowledge

2=Wisdom

3=Understanding

4=Culture

5=POWER

6=Equality

7=NATURE/UNIVERSE

8=Build or Destroy

9=Born

The numerology, as above, has already been laid down by Islam and the attributes have been assigned to each number for the purpose of pure understanding. Leroy Walker was greeted by the Muslims, since he scored unexceptionally well on all the attributes stated above and has therefore been regarded as a "10 percent wizard" by several Nations of the religion Islam. He received a full score of 10, since he was able to practice everything that was taught to him. Not only this, he used his experience to monitor and change the lives of others. It is important for you to note here that "Walker" is neither a Muslim by religion, nor a man of religion. He merely has an x-factor associated with him personality, which we all can find in ours if we make attempts like he did.

*Narrator: - The narrator of all the lessons that has been sent to mankind is an entity who has full control on us. It controls our blessings, which essentially are the products of our own actions. Human beings, through their actions have full control on either deny the blessings that have been sent down to him or to embrace them with open arms. Remember the fact that our actions have a great impact on our lives. Walker has observed this phenomenon personally and would like to share his experience for the betterment of entire mankind.

Walker wants you to comprehend the "cycle of understanding", under which he affirms that

"A human must recognize what is around him and it can only come with acute observation. Try to sharpen your focus and when you are able to understand the truth, hold its value since it would help you to become wiser"

* Narrator: Remember that I have used started explaining the cycle of understanding.

(Leroy Walker)

"3rd Degree understanding of reality of numerology"

0= Remember that nothingness is the ultimate truth. Before this universe, there was nothing and once the climax of this universe has been announced, there would be nothing. I suggest that everyone must become self-aware before they start to spread the information about them to others. The number zero, however, is the reality of mankind and this universe. Even drawing a number zero is interesting. The lines we draw to write 'zero' displays the intentions behind writing this number down and the colour of the ink demonstrates the reality associated with the number. The mix of reality and intentions provides meaning to the number zero.

Example: Primary colours are mixed together to

make one or more colours. You blend in different realities to create a new reality with an entirely different meaning. Another example in this regard can that be of a baby. Mother and father, being two different individuals, give birth to an entirely new human being and this is exactly like creating a new reality However this number signifies one's own thoughts, choices, plots, plans, intentions and ingredients before any act, is involved. It also symbolizes any creativity that makes sense, to reality. This number symbolizes the uncertainty associated with life and its circumstances.

1= Gaining knowledge in the best possible way.

2= Knowledge makes you wise and once you are wise, you are able to make informed decisions.

3= After practicing the power of your knowledge with good decision making, you would become truthful and would understand the importance of truthfulness in your life.

4= Once you've reached this level of understanding, It is then, that you should prepare it, to give, and to let grow within your surroundings. If acknowledged and valued, by others, it will grow, because in due time, it will become well recognized by your friends, family, culture, creed, "NATION", or even better, "THE WORLD", depending on the influences you carry, throughout your actions, and approach. You will then become a light bringer in this way of life, or the reviser, of such an understanding

5= Spreading your wisdom among the people would be considered a kind act of charity and would help you to connect with them at emotional level. You would come to understand the natures of your fellow humans and would soon be able to share your values in life with them. As they grow, with your help, they would make decisions that would be influenced by your teachings and you would find intrinsic satisfaction in this. The readiness to teach other would grant you eternal peace and you would soon cherish your abilities to impact the lives of others.

7= This process would either make people love you, or they may envy or hate you. Whatever the circumstances maybe, you should not stop giving away to people. You have to become a leader and this may make you obnoxious among people, but you have to do it under all circumstances or you would lose number 8.

8= At this level, you is either to build or destroy the intentions of a certain reality, or the values of a certain reality by all means.

This number symbolizes a pressure point, being

placed into reality that all must encounter, before moving on, and the coming of its existence is quite "Natural".

If you break down,(become destroyed) you may become lost; but if you would build from a sharp focus, you will then start to see things more differently, and with this, comes more truths, and so comes the light, quite Naturally).

9= This number comes handy, when your mind, body and spirit have now being built with number 8. You would enter a new world of understanding from here onwards and you would notice the numbers double from here on.

"ANGELS OF THE LIGHT"

Founded by: Mr. Leroy Walker
"There will be Robes made for all shapes, and sizes; For Every Branch of this Order that will be represented by the People, of every nation, that comes to join us, in our involvement for a New Kingdom, Here on Earth; Blessed Be.

*The Light House- "The main House", governed by Mr. Walker and the Shape Shifters, from all over the Globe.

*The House of 144,000- "There will be as many as 144000 watch-out nations in the world, which would be scattered disharmoniously around the globe and the people in need would sound help from them." This means that in times of need, people would seek help from these nations instead of referring back to their own governments or their own mayors. The officials from whom the help would be sought would ask the representative nations about the problems and shortages in their areas. The document stating the shortages and difficulties would then be sent to helping nations and they would be known as the "House of needs".

*The House of Needs- This house is where all the missions, and different objectives, will be given to the Angels, and the different Branches that they are of.

If the complaint is about feed, then this house will establish the mission, date, and time, for the presence, of the Angels, to come and get things right.

The moral to this house, is this: "There's no job to big, that The Angels can't handle."

12 Jewels of accomplishments, to come to past, as our main goal, that is inevitable; that these jewels will then be free of charge, for the better:

1. Free Knowledge

2. Free Wisdom

3. Free Understanding- Make sure that you have full understanding of all the underlying values of truth and righteousness

4.Real Freedom

5.Real Justice

6.Real Equality

7. Real, and Free Food

8.Free Clothes

9.Free Shelter

10. The influence of pure love, which will awake, from the acts of sudden shifts.

11.Peace will be carefully watched, and protected, by the house of 144,000.

12. This will all add up, and equal out, to complete Happiness, for each and every individual.

*The House of Angels- This house will be of the muscle, "The People"; from every nation, and field of mankind.

*Mother's of The World:- This Branch of Angels, will be the eye over the children of the world, Which are those, that are branched, from "The House Of 144,000".

That when shelter is given, they sit around to make sure, that no more is needed.

When Food is given, they sit around, and make sure that no more is being needed.

They will also have the authority to demand.

They will be under Oath, to adopt the World, care for the world, as if it was their own new born. This branch will have a split ;(One side is for the Humans, and the other is for the animals).

*NEED TRUST ORGANIZATIONS.- This organization would be the sub-branch of the "House of needs". It will place currency with the stock exchange, which in turn would manifest in into a new order of commitment. The items kept in stock would be products of needs, such as, hygiene products and the products of daily use.

*hospitals would be free of cost. They would not

charge a penny to anyone; let them be in major cities or in minor cities, with the promise of best possible services. This will be governed by The House of Needs (And the rest of this is also top secret and safely secured.)

*Knights of Honour, Feeding Program- Feeding the entire world, the best of food, with no strings attached, no risks involved, with food health, (such as mad cow disease,) and etc. "My Knights brand of food will be from the Beginning to End, of a marvellous preparation and if the food source in the future depletes, you would find yourself a huge safe to fee everyone. This would also be free of cost.

This is just another branch, of "The House of Needs."- (The secret of it is also concealed for the time being)

*Knights of Honour, Sheltering Program- Same method as the Feeding Program, but in place of food, free shelter is the promise here

*The Knights of Honour, This knight of honour promises free clothes to people in times of dire need.

*Peace Parkers- Peace parkers would be special people who would help sign peace pacts between two rival nations by setting up terms of bargain. They would remove tensions from the world by offering the rivals with offers that would be too tempting to

resist.

Facebook Social Networking: The page "angels of light" has been created on Facebook to draw the attention of the masses towards it. The page would soon launch recruitment portal for the people, who are ready to work for the welfare of the mankind.

To all the people who want to become as righteous as an angel, following are some of the guidelines that would help you to adopt angel like traits and characteristics.

An angel like human is the one who thinks about nothing, but for the welfare of the mankind. You would be considered as an angel by others if, the food you offer to the needy is free, the shelter is proper for them and does not include any charges and the health and healing of all kinds do not ask for monetary charges.

The person or organization, which promises to posses angel-like traits, must take care of all of the humanity, regardless of their cast or creed. An unmarked promise to the mankind must be adopted.

Once these angels have taken over the world, with their wide-spread acts of kindness, the world would be a free place. It would be a holy kingdom, where the necessities of life are free of charge. Once the world learns to engage with these angels, apart from physical commodities, several other things would also be free, which includes respect, love, kindness and mercy.

Find your own interest in treating others with respect; a) if you want to feel a hungry person, take a step right now and provide them with best food and become a beacon of light and ray of hope for the world. b) If you are a carpenter and can build even a small home for a needy person, contact us and we would consider you as a part of a helping muscle. We are interested in recruiting people from all fields who are dedicated to mankind and are ready to make a change on global level. So, all of you are encouraged to join our cause, as far as you have a kind heart and you are resolute to make a change for the sake of humanity.

Once you are ready to help the humanity, you will soon start to see the change and you would love to see the impact you have made for the welfare of humanity.

Note:

There are many Gurus working for the welfare of humanity and only a few of them can truly succeed. My works intends to encourage of human lovers to join hands with me, so that we can turn this world into a palate of peace for grieve-stricken people. I would make attempts to learn from them and they can take good values from me, if they think I am good enough. I am just a step towards a glorious future.

The angels created through this process would fix the problems in this would, would bring people together in the mutual bond of love and would teach them harmony and peace. A chief of declaration is an important piece, prepared by me in three sections, which I would share with you through this book.

Section one: *For the government officials*: Government officials must make attempts to recruits those 'angels' who are ready to work for the welfare of the mankind.

Section two: *For the officials of recruitment*: Applications must be floated in the entire country for people to become the part of a social cause that would serve the humanity. This would be done by officials of recruitment, hired by the government. This would serve two purposes. First, unemployed people would get jobs; second, these recruiters would serve humanity, free of any intrinsic motives and hence would be useful to spread love around the world. Also, government must promise them privileges, better than military since they are striving for the welfare of the entire mankind.

Section three: *For the servers*: The servers must take a vow to serve the entire humanity regardless of the cast or creed of people.

Also, the peace-makers, discussed above in the book would deal with the tensions of the world, by making peace between the rival nations.

The group page for the angels of light can be

found   at:
https://www.facebook.com/groups/3811885919446
24/

Join the group to be a part of this cause.   The
representatives would get in direct contact with you.

"THE PROMISE"

I say unto every nation, that the time is almost near. Soon I will help all to realize, what they had been longing for, this entire time. I say to all that really want to see this planet mould into a just world, that it is for you to get well prepared and passionate enough for what's about to come.

If you wish to secure the future of your generations and are desperate to save them from the wrath of the future wars, then come, stand by me. If you are tired of wars, no matter how deep it may seem in your country, tired of having endless enemies out to kill you and your future (children), then spread the word about me, to your people, and get prepared to come stand by me; If you are willing to love your enemies 1st., making peace out of respect for yourself and others, so that enemies could soften up their hearts about you, becoming later friends and family with once rivals, then it is for you to come stand by me. If you are tired of starving, tired of watching your people starve, along with people of the world, tired of slaving for little, or nothing then come stand by me. If you are tired of being treated as the last in the row, since you have little or no leadership skills, then stand by me. I will teach you the way to take over the world and would provide you a special blueprint, which you would treat as a guide from heavens.

When I speak, I speak on behalf of all of the people, from all of the Nations, which means I am an orator for humanity. My first step to bring people on the path of truth would be, to publish this book as a guide and to reveal how a new kingdom is on its way. Any government or any other kingdom which attempts to oppose me would soon reveal itself as a Kingdom of enemy. However, I promise to be a source of relief for all the nations. Do not fear my motives, since I am only here to make this world a better place for living. I would serve your nation, its economy and its trade for free. I, along with my healers, would soon come to your Nation to reveal you from all kinds of hardships and suppression. I would re-define the economic parameters of your country, which would strengthen your economy in a sustainable manner. It is my promise that my use of values would revive progress and growth in your country. What I ask in return is not a monetary benefit, but a request to all of you to become a part of my healing organization i.e. "The Angels". I would elaborate the motive behind this organization in great detail once I visit your land. Peace should be eternal and we all have to make cohesive attempts to surrender to a peaceful world.

"Letter to All Nations"

In order to have a peaceful agreement with a rival Nation, you must first offer some lucrative terms to them, which they cannot refuse. You must start by developing cordial relationships with the people of your rival states. Interact with them on friendly terms and tell them how you are on their side and how your people also support your motive. Let them know that you and your people had chosen to love them, from this point on, and for them to also let the past remain the past, for the sake of the children being of both, or all parties involved. In order for me and the Angels to bring about free food, shelter, clothes, healing, and also to implant the genuineness of peace, love, and happiness you all must become willing to help us bring forth a major relief to your land, no matter the cost of self pride, that this effort be the sacrifice, for a brighter future, being made by all, and it all starts here. Do this for the sake of your future generations, for your friends and for the betterment of your beloved family.

When we come to your land, we would greet you with open arms, would join hands with you and would treat you like brothers and sisters, for this is what we are for each other. It is now time to strive for harmony and peace and also to employ ways that are best for humanity. My master plan is comprehensive and would be used to bring people together. I am already in love with my followers and soon you would also learn the world of love and would become affectionate towards your enemy even. I and my angels would get together to help this world become a better place.

If you hope for a peaceful world, then come and stand by me. If you want to be the part of the organization named, The Angels, then I assure you that you would get several opportunities to be a part of this wonderful organization.

"Relief and peace would prevail in this world, with hard work and sacrifices"

Afghanistan- To your land I will bring economic guarantees, free food, shelter, clothes, and those that are able to heal. Out of your land, as well as all others, I will take one person and make him a "Peace Parker" while recruiting many others to become Angels, to help make things right in your land, as well as in all other Nations. Children are to live their lives with a decent childhood. We will also bring about peace between you and your rivals. I want for you and your children to live a healthy life style without having to watch out for enemies. All of this will be for you, and your children to become able to live in complete happiness, for the rest of time. All I want in return is to be able to recruit many of you into this new organization. I will speak on it more, when I arrive, but also I want for you to be willing to settle against the act of war, so that you could enjoy this new lifestyle. We all as a world will soon have to surrender to peace and make relief. Oh' what a wonderful feeling.

Albania: O' People of Albania, I consider it as my duty to come and visit you and to help you in all kind of situations. I would make attempts to make your lives more liveable by softening the hearts of your leaders. To the government of Albania, I promise to provide a formula through which your people would fall in love with you all over again. All your people desire is fairness and justice. If they see would be able to see the endeavours, you have put in for their betterment, they would shed the tears of joy and would accept you their Kings and queens with all their hearts. I would only visit your land, as a friend and a facilitator, since a helper must be genuine and dedicated towards the cause of the people. I would also help to uplift the failing morals of people. As far as the leaders of Albania are concerned, I promise to make them better, even if it means bribing them with money or morality. I promise to fix the economy of your land, and introduce a free-market system where basic necessities of lives are free of cost. My major objective is to fulfil all your needs and to help flourish peace and love in your land. I promise, I would be coming really soon.

Algeria- All you ever wanted was to be free from war, free from hate and I understand that you have invested a lot of energies to have peace in your land. If you feel devastated due to the consequences of the war, this is where I come in, bringing peace between you and your rivals. Sounds impossible? Well I already have a plan. Not only that, but I'm a fix it to where this problem never happens again. I love you and you will soon love me too. I will come to do great favours and would provide you relief, following the sane action plan as laid for Afghanistan. I love you all and I cannot wait to meet you soon.

Andorra- I am resolute to grant your basic needs, once I visit your land. Once I am done with my exercise of healing, there would be no chaos left on your land and peace would prevail. Like all the other countries discussed above, my objective to visit your land would be to end war, provide peace and shelter to the people of your land. This address is just a way to send warm greetings, your way, before I actually visit you.

Before I proceed any further, I would like to clear that although I am addressing every nation separating for the purpose of personalizing my message, I would like you to know that I would not treat one nation different than the rest. All would receive equal treatment of love and care under the common umbrella of humanity. I want to address the unique problems of every state so that they can connect with me and can know that I have got empathy for them and their problems.

Angola- You have got plenty of problems, like the rest of the states, but we will get together and find a way forward. I cannot wait to shed my love on you and your children. My forces of Angels, coming from different nations, would be the part of this noble cause, the objective of which is to serve the humanity. I promise to fulfil your needs, I take a pledge to end your all miseries and I promise to reinvigorate your economy for the purpose of future resource sustainability. We will be in every nation, soon, recruiting more helpers (Angels) for the ride. I can't wait to come, and give the ultimate helping hand, to your people. I love you, and you will soon learn to love your enemies, because after my arrival, you will cease to have them. Oh' what a wonderful feeling.

Antigua and Barbuda- Greetings to the twin Island! I have observed that you have got limited supply of fresh water, which cannot be absorbed by the soil, since due to deforestation, the water runs down the slopes of the land and into the sea. The heavy flow of water leads to soil erosion, which in turns reduces the fertility of the soil, hence making the growth of vegetation difficult. Once the soil is infertile, trees would not grow in that land and similar has happened to your island. The lowering of soil and vegetation has led to acidic rain, which is dangerous for plants, humans and animals. We must find a plausible solution for this. I, along with my Angels, would visit your land and would make sure to plant trees so as to stabilize the environment and hence the climate of the area. This is turn would provide you with fresh water in the future. The access to fresh water and food, from our side would be free of cost. Every Angel, along with me, would make sure that you are a part of a better and peaceful world, where availability of fresh water is no more a problem.

Anyone can become a part of my organization; provided, they have sufficient urge to serve the humanity. Being humans you must realize that trees are an essential part of the ecosystem and moderate the climate of the world. Try to have a balance in cutting and plantation of the trees. I understand that you need to build up infrastructure for growth and survival of your economy, but they must also be replanted so as to have a harmonious balance with the nature. It is important for you to know, that whatever we take away from Mother Nature, it must be returned back to it. I am not a person of words, who just preaches you about an ideal situation. I am here to motivate you to take an action for the sake of your country and your people. I love you all and that we Angels will be in your land, to aid you all shortly. So make note of any other problems before we arrive, so that your land, people, and animals could become settled.

Argentina- I promise to provide you with shelter and homes that would not fall off from storms. Remember that I love you and my love for you would be unconditional, like it is for other Nations.

The path of righteousness is the path to eternity. If you are righteous, we would soon complete our objectives in your nation.

Armenia- We (as The Angels) shall also come to your land with opened arms. We will come to strengthen your economy, right along with all other set problems that you all have currently. You all are known to be very friendly people, and right where you stand, today, is where most of "The Angels" will soon come from, for the sake of the entire world. So, take heed and get ready for my arrival.

Australia- We will come to upgrade your environment by striving to cure the impacts of nuclear proliferation on environment. We would take suggestions from the scientists, who would be recruited in our force of angels. Along with upgrading the environmental elements, I promise to remove the anomalies of your economic situations as well, as I do it with any other country. I love you, and hope for you all the best. I will be there to visit, and to also help work these issues out. Remember that we all are one, and that we all must soon come together, one way or the other. This is my plan for you Australia, and you too will gain great benefits from "The Angels", so get ready to be changed for good.

Austria- You are facing the similar issues, as that of Antigua & Barbuda (read what I have told Antigua and Barbuda about their current issues. The remedy I have proposed to them would also be applicable in your case. If you have any other issues, list them down, since I would address them once I visit your land with my Angels. Keep your heads up, smile, and just know that a better future is on its way. Other than that, feeding, sheltering, clothing and free heal and health facilities are yet some other promises for the people of your land. My main goal is to improve your lives in the best possible ways.

Azerbaijan- No matter how intense is your problem; I, with the help of my Angels, would take care of it. We are determined to help the mankind and all you have to do is to have faith on the purity of our intentions and to wait for us. We promise to arrive on hummers, choppers, vans and 18 wheelers to help you out. I love you all, always will, and we are destined to succeed.

Bahamas- I understand how you feel about disagreeing with the U.S. on the alignment of the northern axis, of a potential maritime boundary. I am only a man of love, wisdom, solutions and a kind of helping hand, who is here to help and teach you all. I empathize with you and your feelings. Once I visit your land, I promise to spread the message of love that would end all street-demonstrations, would help the poor and the needy and would fulfil the emotional, psychological and basic needs of the humans. It is vital that you are well-aware of all your problems when I visit you, so that, I can comprehensively address them, with the help of my Angels. Why? Well, because I love you, and I only want the best for you. Other than that, I will come to enjoy my vacation(s) in the Bahamas.

Bahrain- I am able to observe religious violence, as a part of several issues, which have destroyed the peace and harmony in your land. Many of you are waiting for an Imam Mahdi, who would solve all of the problems of the people in the world, and would help establish eternal peace. I do not claim to be your Imam, but I would make legitimate endeavours to ascertain that the peace is prevalent in all of the nations of the world. I would make attempts to provide a better standard of living to all people of the world, regardless of their gender, caste, religion or creed. The hungry would get food, the homeless would be provided shelter and the poor would be blessed with my love. I love you all so much that I would make multiple sacrifices to help you all succeed. I understand that your God, being Allah, is all Merciful and therefore, He would be delighted to see this world in state of perfect harmony and peace. I do not want you to give away your lives in needless wars; I want you to survive, with a better promise of things in life. Do not let people, with negative energies to deviate you from right path. Be resolute and have faith in yourself and trust me that I would put in every possible effort to make this world a superior place for you.

Bangladesh- The good thing about you and your nation is that you are making efforts to become self-sufficient. You are not dependent upon any other nation and have faith in your abilities. I would appreciate your this approach and would advise other nations to follow your suit. But even then, I promise to visit your land to make matters even better. Because of your dedicated, intellectual and future-oriented leaders, you have progressed a lot, but there is still a way to go for you. I plan to setup orphanages in your land, in order to provide shelter to destitute and parentless children. I and "The Angels" will come to aid you, feeding all, sheltering all, clothing all, and to help heal all people, places, and things. If you or any other person, from this nation (or any other nation) want to become an "Angel", then soon you would see many avenues to avail this opportunities.

Barbados- Barbados is suffering from environmental degradation due to pollution. The major type of pollution in Barbados is water pollution, which has taken place since the ships have spilled wastes in the water for a longer period of time, which has led to the contamination of water. But if the water sources have been smeared, it does not mean the end of the world. I promise to address this issue too, with the help of my learned Angels. I hope that with my help and with the help of my

Angels, several issues in your state would be solved. I have great regard for your singer Rihanna, but I have equally great regard for all of you and therefore, I am coming to make your country an even better place to live.

Since there are so many nations which I plan to visit and turn them into hubs of peace and harmony, I would now make an attempt to shorten my note down. To the Middle East, I promise peace to your people and a state of harmony for your government. I already have followers and partners in Iraq and Jordan, who once came to me for help and then succeeded in achieving their goals. My partners have spread the message about my powers of love and kindness, across the boarders and therefore, the people of Iraq are earnestly waiting for me. They want me to visit Iraq and make it a better place for their children, family and their future generations. The people of Iraq are ready to forgive its enemy and rivals for the sake of eternal peace and harmony, since it is an ultimate truth about the world.

I already have a partner in Iraq, and Jordan that have already approached me about their issues, and that the Iraqi people are all waiting on me to come help make their place a better place to be, for the sake of the children, people, love, and future. The people of Iraq are now willing to forgive their rivals, allowing the past to remain the past, that in reality once rivals will soon become family and friends. We love you Iran, and that we all shall make this surrender from such hate, and war, in trade for peace and a relief. We are the advocates of peace and building each and other would give us peace of mind and purity of soul. I aim to spread my message of love and affection throughout the Middle East. My objective is to make them brothers and to remove enmity from among them. Once they have learnt from me, they would eventually make attempt to represent me, like my other fellows from Jordon. I feel, I would be a part of a new brotherhood, for which I consider myself as lucky.

My message of love and peace is for all of the Nations, including; Belarus, Belgium, Belize, Bhutan, Bolivia, Bosnia & Herzegovina, Botswana, Brazil, Brunei, Bulgaria, Burkina Faso, Burundi, Cambodia, Cameroon, Canada, Cape Verde, Central African Republic, Chad, Chile, China, Columbia, Comoros, Congo, Costa Rica, Cote D'lvoire, Croatia, Cuba, Cyprus, Czech Republic, Democratic People's Republic of Korea, Democratic Republic of The Congo, Denmark, Djibouti, Dominica, Dominican Republic, Ecuador, Egypt, El Salvador, Equatorial Guinea, Eritrea, Estonia, Ethiopia, Fiji, Finland, France, Gabon, Gambia, Georgia, Germany, Ghana, Greece, Grenada, Guatemala, Guinea, Guinea-Bissau, Guyana, Haiti, Honduras, Hungary, Iceland, India, Indonesia, Iran, Iraq, Ireland, Israel, Italy, Jamaica, Japan, Jordan, Kazakhstan, Kenya, Kiribati, Kuwait, Kyrgyzstan, Laos, Latura, Lebanon, Lesotho,

Liberia, Libya, Liechtenstein, Lithuania, Luxembourg, Madagascar, Malawi, Malaysia, Maldives, Mali, Malta, Marshall Islands, Mauritania, Mauritius, Mexico, Micronesia, Moldova, Monaco, Mongolia, Montenegro, Morocco, Mozambique, Myanmar, Namibia, Nauru, Nepal, Netherlands, New Zealand, Nicaragua, Niger, Nigeria, Norway, Oman, Pakistan, Palau, Panama, Papua New Guinea, Paraguay, Peru, Philippines, Poland, Portugal, Qatar, Republic of Korea, Romania, Russia, Rwanda, Saint Kitts &Nevis, Saint Vincent & The Grenadines, Samoa, San Marino, Sao Tome & Principe, Saudi Arabia, Senegal, Serbia, Seychelles, Sierra Leone, Singapore, Slovakia, Slovenia, Solomon Islands, Somalia, South Africa, Spain, Sri Lanka, Sudan, Suriname, Swaziland, Sweden, Switzerland, Syria, Tajikistan, Tanzania, Thailand, The former Yugoslav, Republic of Macedonia, Timor-Leste, Togo, Tonga, Trinidad & Tobago, Tunisia, Turkey, Turkmenistan, Tuvalu, Uganda, Ukraine, United Arab Emirates, United Kingdom, United States, Uruguay, Uzbekistan, Vanuatu, Venezuela, Vietnam, Yemen, Yugoslavia, Zaire, Zambia & Zimbabwe, I shall and will come to aid you all.

"SPIRITUAL TEACHINGS"

Greetings to the Esoteric World!

I would use the power of the spiritual teachings in the same way as people use martial arts. The mighty spiritual learning must not be used for a negative purpose, since it is a type of energy, the use of which must be well articulated and hence properly understood.

The practice of using these teachings at the right time would sharpen your natural and analytical skills; therefore, I have made an attempt to pass this knowledge on to you.

We would start from the very basics and once you are able to capture the crux of the lesson, I would impart more knowledge to you. I would share this knowledge in bits and pieces, so that, you may not feel over-whelmed. I would start with the very fundamentals so that the lesson makes sense to you.

I have been a spiritual teacher for a very long time, so if you have any questions regarding my beliefs or practices, feel free to present them to me.

I would like to tell you here, that there is no specific need for materialistic talismans, since I will teach you the method to charge the spirit in a natural and a real manner. I would teach you the art of synchronizing your brain with positive energy, so that you can have a positive frame of mind, which is vital to learn this method.

The spiritual connection between once mind and the eternal peace within self is vital to understand the truths if this mysterious world.

In order to be happy, surround yourself with positive objects that radiate positive energy. This energy must eventually radiate from within you.

I would now introduce you to the alpha level of understanding. You all must have heard of it, but only a few of you would actually understand the real meaning of it. There is a high possibility that you must have been introduced to the alpha level of understanding, but you would seldom be completely acquainted with it. Majority of the esoteric teachers today, expect you to completely understand the meaning of their entire knowledge talk. They make use of the diagrams, missing out absolute details and expect you to give closure yourself. The problem is that not everyone is sufficiently brilliant to grasp all concepts quickly, as they come their way. Therefore, I promise to offer a comprehensive method of teaching that would place you in the centre of your alpha and would help you learn.

A major tool required to ensure the success of your students is to spend maximum time with them so that their level of understanding can improve. I will teach my students to make peace in the mind and to have mental control over difficult situations and hence find solutions to minor and major problems.

In order to have a positive solution to your problem, I request you to nourish your mind with the positive energy of healthy thoughts, which in turn would trigger an emotional and hence a spiritual relief. By keeping positive about all the circumstances on hand, you would get eternal peace of mind in a natural manner.

If all of the people in the world would adopt a positive and constructive approach to their problems, they would become mentally strong. Their determination to sublime their hardships with the help of positive energy would put them on the path of success and righteousness. This in turn would put you on the path of spiritual progress and hence would strengthen the spiritual senses of the human beings. After adopting this method, to counter their problems, people would find a degree of everlasting eternal peace in them and this feedback from the body would grant them confidence on themselves. Such people would become emotionally and physically strong in the face of all of the crisis or difficulties.

The method of warding off evil, by staying optimistic in all circumstances has been personally used by me and I promise you my dear students that it will eventually benefit you as well.

Always remember, there is no need to master the art of self- control within a limited period of time. Do not be very harsh on yourself. You would eventually become a self-restraint person, once you have started to put in honest efforts into changing yourself. Approach your problem tactfully and find a solution using the power of your mind.

You may not know what I am doing as a mentor here, but I know the importance of this exercise, which eventually would benefit the humanity as a whole. Use nature as your guide to help you make right decisions. Trust your intuition and use your thoughts, ideas and gut-feeling as support tools in events of difficulty. The harmony of thoughts, actions and feelings can help you become organized as a spiritual human being, who is ready to embrace the truth of the world.

If any other master of spiritual therapy is reading this work of mine, they must realize that I am not forcing any of my followers to change as a person. I want them to stay the way they are, and just change the way they think. It comes without saying that a person has to be his real self while accepting a message or a theory; otherwise, he would not able to dedicate himself to the cause or the idea behind the cause. A person who stays truthful to the self and does not adopt the art of pretence to impress anybody, would accept my message whole-heartedly and his energy would be observable by the onlookers. This person would radiate positive energy since this energy would not only be genuine but would be the true reflection of his heart and soul. Eventually, understanding the importance of faithfulness and in turn, realizing the importance of purity of the spirit, these people would adopt righteousness as a way of their life. After a certain period of time, they would become masters themselves.

If my students would have any questions for me, I would be more than happy to address them in great detail so as to enable them to have a spiritual revival. The first step on the path of righteousness is to get rid of all of the pessimism from your life. Break the barriers which would stop you from practicing esoteric arts. The practice of special spiritual powers or the esoteric arts was made difficult for the people, who wanted to change the world with their power of purity. However, I promise, under my guidance, the pursuit of truth would be effortless.

For the time being, I want my students to practice what I give to them, with all their hearts. They must stay truthful and I do not expect them to change their original selves in the process. Once they follow my lessons, they change in them would not only be positive, but it would be original.

My dear students from all over the world! I want you to realize that meditation does not being still, or having a blank mind. These are the lies, you would hear from those, who not want you to learn the underlying values of it. Meditation concerns thinking and dwelling. Or, for the purpose of clarity, I would say that meditation is synonymous to dwelling.

One of the most intriguing questions that come in the mind of the people, who are on a spiritual journey is, *"what can be done to contemplate or dwell about something"?*

The very simple answer to this question is that meditation or dwelling is a natural phenomenon. The desire or the urge to meditate comes naturally in a human being when he wants to envision the hidden truths of the world. Ask yourself questions like as to why I want to meditate? What would be the points of contemplation during my meditation and how good I am in reasoning or applying logic to the things? Once you know what drives your desire to meditate, the entire process would soon become self-explanatory.

Contemplating over a complex situation for the considerable period of time would help you find answers, which otherwise would be difficult to find. I advise you to pay close attention to the problems around you, in order to get answers.

In order to make the world a better place for others and for your own-self, I suggest you to follow the above given lesson with determination and resolution.

Intuitions*

Intuition is the natural tool that humans can use in their pursuit of truth. Nature has bestowed humans with intuition, so that in the times of mystification and bewilderment, where they are unable to seek help from others, their intuitions can serve as a guide for them. Your intuitions would guide you on the path of truth and would be your mentor in the times of solitude. Intuitions guide you under all situations, in all places and under all scenarios. Most of the times, you would either not be able to listen to your intuition or you would not follow them since you would present a logic that they do not demonstrate real facts. As a human, in the pursuit of truth, you must never ignore your intuitions since they are the angelic masters, guiding you on the right path. They are the gift of the nature to the mankind. If you want to be successful on your journey of spirituality, your inner energies must be in complete synchronization with your intuitions.

The search for truth must be meaningful and mature. Truth is invincible and when you would be on the right path, seeking the light of truth, intuitions would be your close companion. Sometimes, the truth is so harsh that you want to deviate from it and would like to choose an alternate path, which would be comparatively less complicated and less harsh. When you will be taking an alternate path, ignoring the truth, your intuitions would force you to stay on the right way. Once you listen to your intuitions and adopt the path of light again, you would no longer be regarded as being astray, since getting lost on the path of truth is the part of journey.

Since your intuitions would always be your guide on the path of righteousness, you would soon learn to listen to them under all circumstances.

Intuitions would eventually make you aware about your own negative or positive energies. Once you start listening to them, they would eventually become stronger and would become your ultimate companion over the years. Once your inner energies are bonded with your intuition, you would feel your intuitions getting stronger. In order to master the art of taking help from your intuition, you must first master predictive art i.e. you must be aware of all of the situations in which you are in. Once you have complete information about your surrounding circumstances, the flaws would eventually be evident themselves and your intuitions would help you solve the problems, with dignity and perfection. The continuous struggle with identifying and exploiting your intuitions would eventually make them sharper and stronger. They would subsequently become your natural mentor at all times. Acute observation, with the desire to learn is another way to sharper your intuitions.

Let us practice this phenomenon of listening first, which in turn would sharpen your intuition.

Listen to the voice, deep down inside you. What does it tell you about the situation in which you are in and about your future in general?

Try to get an answer from deep down. Practice this ritual daily to listen to your inner voices more clearly. Do this exercise, in order to understand, how well of a guide your intuitions are. Get aware about the type of intuitions you have. They may be mild or strong, depending upon the importance you have given to them in the past. As you become more aware about yourself, gain control on your surroundings and know your situations well, you would eventually become more aware about the self. Awareness, in turn, would strengthen your intuitions. You must be careful while looking for your intuitions from within. Every opinion is not intuition and every set of belief does not determine the values of your intuitions. In order to know them better, you have to dig deep inside and concentrate with full commitment.

Nature will always leave clues, and from this, the universe will know where you stand, if you are ready for certainty, and so forth. The better you become, at being aware, figuring things out, knowing how to go and get what is needed to complete a puzzled situation, it is then that the universe will give you more of what is needed for the ride, in addition. You would then grow into a much keener sense of awareness, which would soon lead you towards more truths, to grow from. Listening to the self, and searching to find truth, for a relief, be the bonding stage(s), between the self, and that inner voice that lets you know, that something isn't right or the fact that it is incomplete.

Listen with dedication and never ignore what the little inner voice tells you, since in this way, you might eventually kill it. You must understand the ups and downs in the way of self-actualization, which would be of great help for your intuition.

Intuition is not an imagination, it is an undeniable truth. In order to see it properly, you must have faith in its existence. Knowing what to do, and how to do it, to find out the truth, for a final relief, should be the goal, in this case. Become skilled in this, by becoming skilled in finding your sources, that will give your inner self relief from all that worrying.

"SPIRITUAL CHARITY"

There is as much commotion in the spiritual world as it is in the living world. Spiritual beings gain so much more access, on changing the vibe of life, that surrounds the living, let alone fix things that is needed to be fixed, as loyal agents of Nature, and all nature asks of them, is to become balanced, That they have a proper influence, to have an impact on the vulnerable, by targeting their mind frame. This vulnerable would not be aware of the control; the spiritual beings have on their mind and body.

Nature draws a well defined line between the physical being and the dead and in turn the spiritual beings. Living has to perform numerous tasks on daily bases. They would be held accountable for their actions, in a positive or negative manner. Living makes multiple choices in their lives, which in collaboration with the work of nature, determines their fate. The fate in turn influences their living patterns. A person with good conduct comes in perfect harmony with the nature and the nature is indebted to bless him. These blessings are in material form for the living.

As for the dead spiritual souls, they would help me to identify the needy and to provide them with food and shelter.

They would lead me to the miserable and hungry ones, who want to hide from the eye of the merciless world.

Patterns would fall in pieces, with the help of the spiritual dead and the living need not to them of their existence or about their help. The dead would help to have this world in perfect synchronization with the peace and harmony

(Leroy Walker)

Let me add up the entire lesson to you for your better understanding,

When I say, I want to pass on my services; I say it with good intentions and for the betterment for the humanity as a whole.

I do not only eat the food but I enjoy it, since I am dedicated towards a noble cause. Moreover, I am peaceful since nature supports my actions and intentions.

I do the right thing, in the right situations i.e. the energy I ward off is always positive and is in complete synchronization with the rituals of the nature.

It is important for you to know that dead have intentions as well and they do also enjoy energy depending upon their intentions. If their intentions are pure, they would be associated with positive energy, but the energy of dead is more passive than the energy of living. They also handle multiple duties in the world, depending upon the directions they decide to follow.

Nature has a perfect mechanism of supply and demand i.e. if you decide to help someone by giving away food to them, the nature would bless you even double and the food you get would come with satisfaction and pleasure now.

Sometimes, I get to answer the questions like, How long have you been giving away to people and what makes you so passionate about humanity and why you want to give back to them.

Leroy Walker:

"I had been doing this since forever. Now look at the results that I am now one elite agent of "Nature's Call", that existence is based on the focus, and the focus makes all things better for human kind, and much more."

*Narrator: Perfect example, for this, is called "Being Worthy Enough".

(Leroy Walker)

I want you to create your own passages that will make you feel good about helping all others, in need. You will feel great about using your active and passive energy to help the needy. Make changes to the world, as if you are a God. Strive for the betterment of the world and work hard to prevail peace in this world

I want you all to take the Olara Control that is in this book, look over it, study it, grow into it, by nature, from recognizing where it fits in your everyday life, as you employ what it takes, quite naturally to achieve its values.

"METHODS"

By my deeper understanding of the nature, I have found a new method, which although is a part of nature, but is highly unrecognized. It needs to be studied in greater detail, in order to understand it in a better way.

This method is known as "The Plane of Natural Signs"

Example: This method is functional for both the men and women. I suggest you to first understand this method and after comprehending its usability, make use of it in your daily lives as a "Tool" for personal betterment.

I would now start explaining this method.

Gentlemen! Understand that if you are in a relationship and are cheating your spouse with other women, it is possible for them to find out with the help of nature. She might not have sufficient exposure with men, which would mean that she would not be able to identify their flirtatious manners properly. If this is the case, then she needs to pay a closer attention to the manners and actions of her mate.

The woman, who is being cheated, would find herself to be drawn to other men and would be mesmerized by their flirtatious manners. She might be tempted to cheat on her companion with another man and may not understand the reason behind her new surfacing desires. The change would be by the nature which has intrigued the woman do to the same as her man is doing.

You would feel persuaded and a natural drive to be away from your man under a situation in which he is cheating on you. You might not be aware of his actions, but you will be naturally drawn towards other men.

You might hear yourself acclaim that "I love my spouse, but there is this incomprehensible underlying desire to flirt or have sex with another man and I do not understand my feelings". These feelings are the outcomes of your spouse's actions. He flirts with other women and although you are oblivious of this fact, you would always be drawn to unknown men. The natural cycle of brutal vengeance has been regarded by me as *"The plane of Natural signs"*.

Once you start to have these strange and inexplicable feelings look closely around you for a proper definition. Make attempts to understand the reason behind your evolving emotions. Target the right cause to eliminate the chances of future chaos from your life.

I do not suggest you to accuse anyone yet, since I am still working on the consequences of this method and the way these situations must be handled or approached.

One thing is for sure, that if you are also cheating on your partner, the nature would not do the kind act of whistle blowing in your favour, since this blessing of nature is only reserved for the innocent.

You must recognize that if flirting is a common habit of you and your spouse; you both would be held accountable by nature. The vicious cycle of karma would start, which would result in the annulment of your relationship.

In order to save you from the wrath of nature, I suggest you to do only the right things in life, since in that way you would be rewarded by nature.

Nature is looking at and telling on everyone in this world, in one way, or the other.

My class of geniuses, this theory has four more sub-branches which would guarantee complete proposition. However, it is important that the subject is completely aware of this method, in order to use it properly in the circumstances of need. The nature and hence the universe, would help me in my pursuit of the truth and in guiding all of you on the right path. I am making untiring efforts in understanding the truths of the universe, which I would use to enlighten all of you.

Like all of the above discussed methods, this method would also be a natural one and would help you recognize the call of nature.

The nature has revealed several of its signs to me and has exposed several ways of self-actualization on me, but before I pass on that knowledge to you, I must first exercise it myself. Now I would further explain this theory to you, so that you can progress in your life.

Nature would help me to train all of you and to make you all super humans. Right now, I suggest you to use "Plane of Nature" method as a warning sign. This means that if I would receive some indication from the nature, I would not ignore it, but would consider as a warning alert by Mother Nature. Once I have received a warning signal towards an object, I would direct my attention towards it. The subject in this case in my spouse. I would look for all the unusual occurrences and using my instincts, I would try to reach the root cause. The whistle that has been blown by nature actually means something and would guide me towards the actual problem. This warning my nature is the first ray that would show me the light of the truth

Another evident ray is the "*the words uttered by a*

person"

For Example: Leonardo does not trust his girl at all, but he wants to trust her, since he loves her. But he needs signs to guide him to the reason behind his mistrust for the girl.

He has an argument with her and he tells her how he finds it difficult to trust her. He provides the girl with instances which made him doubt the credibility of her loyalty. She does not accept these accusations.

So time passes by and one day he figures out that his doubts were reality and the mistrust was the alarm by nature.

He recalls his past and recounts the number of times she has lied to him. While reminiscing about his past, he ponders over the exact words he has said to her while having an argument with him. She called him an "Idiot!" (Now I want you all to remember this part).

Time passes by and the things get even worse between the two; however, the girl promises to make things right for the future

Leonardo figures out a new fact about his girl, i.e. whenever he is right in his confrontation about her, he calls him an idiot. He finds a direct association between the voicing of the word and the truth he reveals about her.

The girl does not realize the way he gets a hit about her new ventures. However, Leonardo is aware of the fact that he is only being called an idiot when his girl friend gets defensive and is trying to hide a secret. So, whenever he calls him an idiot, he immediately knows, something is up.

Sometimes, the signs to recognize can be the movement of the body, the anger being shown when the subject is wrong or complete calmness in case of some other people. However, some people might scream out of distress and hurt when they are right, others, may stay calm when they are truthful, since they know they truth would eventually reveal itself. People in this world are different, so they may act differently in face of truthful confrontation. However, physical signs are another ray to figure out the honesty. I suggest you to keep a close check on physical actions of a person, in order to unleash the truth. I would name the verbal and physical signs revealed by the subject as the third ray of the Plane of Nature.

If you want to benefit from this ray, I suggest, you do not reveal your observations to your subject or they would try to conceal the truth from you in future through their lies and disguise.

I do not brag about my values or about my ability to identify the truth. All I want is, for you, to be able to identify the truth as well as I do. You must benefit from my existence and this is my primary motto here.

I intend to help you all for your personal development and I wish love and peace to all of you.

"NATURE'S QUEST FOR RENEWAL"

Facts about Nature: God's true religion, if any, is explained by the "Nature", for we come in direct contact with Nature and hence it is our best mentor. If you want to do anything for religion, by all means, become the image desired, and help one another.

Nature is full of many different intellects, cycles, and abilities, which stands out as the all natural truth, behind reality. The story lines, behind most of these religions, are false, that they all had been created, by taking some form of truth, out of nature, adding to it, a story, then being given to the people, with an image, and morality, of a religious idol, which had been created to only symbolize the truth. For the truth and God had now been framed, by religions, of all kinds, for centuries.

Q: *When I do something like this, will God Almighty bring it all back, on me?*

A: No; when you do something like this, Nature, a.k.a "Karma" will do the hosting.

Religious leaders have created a ruthless concept of revenge which they claim to have invented;

however, this was always the ritual of the nature. They have symbolizes the wrath of karma as a component of religion. Without this glue, religions wouldn't exist. God made nature the way it is, God didn't make religion, nor is he religious, and I said "created image" as in book type, statue type images, which suppose to represent, or be the Supreme Being.

Q: *How would you explain the existence of Bible and its prophecies?*

A: Back then, was just like right now, it was hard to have a belief, into something, without an image,(pretty much like today, with everyday people), because questions would arise, and if questions are being left, unanswered; people would invent their own answers in order to provide closure to the situations on hand. The observant among those are known as Prophets, since they are able to observe and understand the methods of nature. As they can interpret nature and it ways, they claim to know greater truth and are backed by nature. They are resolute to share their learning with the people and are then known as beholders of the revealed works. The knowledge they impart if a part of truth and the other stories we see in Bible are for the purpose of explanation of the truth.

Example: "The Bible"- One writer after another, and on, and on.

   * When these gentlemen, saw the work of those

before them, they had chosen to take their work, and place it with what they felt like was the right place to bring it. Humans are doing that today, with their everyday skills; taking them where they think it would best benefit.

What you bring forth to the light, in not essentially your work. In most of the cases you just have built upon the previous works or are just a narrator of those works. Becoming naturally directed by the passion, of wanting to do so, that by doing so, you will be rewarded (from nature) for your actions, and that this goes for anybody.

Using me for instance, all of this great stuff, that I give, comes from the inner me and I consider myself responsible to pass it on to all of the people.

The lesson here is to explore the best of your abilities and become the truest and the most cherished human being. Learn from the truths of the nature and once you have learned enough, practice the truth to understand it validity. Once you are well-aware about the benefits certain action has brought you, pass it on to your fellow human beings by either reserving the credits for yourself or by passing these credits on to someone else. God is Almighty and All-knowing, he would be interested in knowing the struggle his creation has put into understanding him. Pass all that you have learnt and teach only what has been proven genuine by your practices.

Have you ever wondered why religious idols are still standing symbolically strong? Well, because the religion has handicapped the minds of its followers by fixating them on certain facts. It has become opium for masses and they have lost confidence in self and do not search and question the motives of the rituals that have passed on to them. On the contrary, the religious orthodox must understand that God wants humans to explore the world, have faith in themselves and grow better by learning from our mistakes.

Now is the time to break away from the curse of religion, "Godly favours are done through each other, instead of just giving believable answers, about Idols, and Icons of a traditional past".

All humans, in their own special way, have the ability to figure things out, around them; but it's up to them, with the interest, that they have, for these things to either become recognized, or not.

While many others would just sit back, and await time to reveal the truth (for time will reveal the truth, If you are smart enough to know how to look for them, in due time, signs will lead your intuitions right on track, towards finding the truth out; but if not striven to find, it may just go, for a great period of time, unrevealed. As time passes by, the truth can either come to the light, from an understanding, or it can continue to be covered with more lies, just as well as it being covered with time

Narrator:-The key towards leaving any religion behind is to give all the people ultimate happiness. It is then that they will go for God without religion, because they will not have time for traditions. Then after complete happiness is restored all over the world, over time, man will find no need for the praise of any Supreme Being. The life which would eventually surround them would be so great that the saviours of the world would be respected even by the religious orthodox and by the negative onlookers.

Perfect example: The wraths of Karma have been regarded as the reimbursements from the God's side by the so-called religious scholars. The term God has been used to manipulate the masses and whenever something undesirable happens, the scholars claim "You will reap that you haw sowed for yourself i.e. God would condemn you for your foul acts". It is true that God s a Supreme Being who has created Nature as His sign. Nature has a reaction to all of our actions and therefore monitors our behaviour. Man has forged the concept of Nature and God by self-created religions. Religion separates Nature from God, in a way that it shows that God voluntarily sends blessings or wrath towards us, which actually is nothing, but is a mere reflection of our own actions. God does not want you to chant praises for Him, since he is Almighty and does not require mere recognition. He wants you to decipher the secrets of this Universe and this, in all ways would be true recognition of His efforts.

This is where I come in:

I intend to take the image that people have created of God (lets them be pictures, statue and other traditional way of worshipping), and associating them back to the Nature, so that the people are able to see the whole picture and realize the ultimate truth. The religions people follow are 10% of the actual truth and the real truth is yet to be discovered. Religion does not depict God and Karma is not God, both are the symbols associated with the bigger picture created by God i.e. the Nature around us. I would help the humans to praise nature and be in a perfect harmony with it. Once this has been established, God would be pleased itself.

Nature is related to existence and the existence of human life has brought us here naturally.

Questionnaire: *Why do humans get the right, to make choices, here on Earth, if these choices can sometimes go wrong?*

Answer: Human being has been bestowed by free-will and Nature is ready to handle the intelligence of the humans. The reality is that nature provides every human with equal opportunities to choose between the right path or a path of absolute darkness and despair. Since Nature is all knowing, a man can be either blessed or can be cursed by his own choices. Since you have free will, the choices belong to you and once you have taken an action, you should be ready to handle its consequences.

Man has created the institution of religion with an objective to search for the truth. Although, the purpose was the pursuit of eternal truth, the human got lost somewhere between religious violence and intolerance towards others. God wants the humans to live in perfect harmony and to weave relationship of love and affection with each other. Once humans get tired of an old reality, they come up with the new reality and this is the reason behind evolution of religions in the past. With reference to the evolutionary nature of humans, I suggest that all of the nations of the world must forget their national differences and must be united under the common banner of truth and tranquillity.

Therefore, all the idols of the world must communicate the message of love and peace. Religions must unite people; it should not divide them, since unity and peace is the ultimate message from Creator.

"BECOME YOUR OWN ENERGETIC POLE"

To the top, which is North, I command you all to restore ties among yourselves and come together in a peaceful cycle of harmony.

To the bottom, which is South, I suggest you all to share your resources with all of the individuals of the world. Forgive people, listen to each other and cherish love and virtuousness for the world to become a better place for dwelling.

Now let's begin to pull closer together, becoming one, starting with each individual with this book, because I love you, shall we?

"THE INNER OPENING"

First of all, I would suggest you all to cherish the life that you have got to its fullest, since this is the only life that you would live.

Become a free human being. This is only possible if you relinquish to your wishes and to your desires. Be yourself and know yourself in detail, in order to get eternal peace and to get inner freedom.

Once you have become free in yourself, your imagination will become more creative. Your power to observe would become strong and you would find yourself looking at the truths of this world.

Do not be afraid to be your real-self, even if it means getting unnecessary disapproval from others. This is a valuable step towards self-actualization. Once you are aware of all your needs and desires, you would come to know your real self. Once your real self is exposed to you, you would know what needs to be changed and what needs to be exercised in order to become a true humanitarian.

Once you start to thrive as an original human being, you would get to know the importance of originality in life. The world may offer you all kinds of freedoms, but the real freedom comes from within. In order to be genuinely free, challenge yourself and come out of the trap of self-denial. Denial takes place when you change your personality, in order to get approval from others. Pretence has a negative impact on your personality and it takes away your confidence and discards your reliability as an authentic person. This may also cause you to deviate from your goals.

If your friends, family, spouse and associates pretend to like your forged personality and you make a commitment to live with it, you must be acquainted with the fact that you would not get eternal satisfaction. In an attempt to make others happy, you may lose the colour of your real self and the search for it may go in vain, in the future.

For all those, who have lost their real-self in a pursuit to become someone else, they must immediately start looking for their real self. My dear friends! Learn to praise and cherish your real self, since it is the only way to self-actualization.

Personal freedom is invaluable and therefore, I would make attempts to coach you about the values of freedom. To be free in real terms, start by understanding yourself from the inside. Be honest to yourself and stand against all the odds, in your pursuit for individualism. Meditate, contemplate and ponder over your personality and your inner desires and follow the path that would help you achieve your goal. Remember, there is no alternate to personal freedom and you must make attempts to be free under all conditions.

Example: *Michael Jackson*

He was unable to present his real self while he was practicing with other partners of his.

He had to adjust, to his surrounding situations, without being free and has to be the Jackson; his associated wanted him to be. He then decided to challenge his fears by deciding to unleash his real-self, and all of a sudden he said, "*I want to try something new and I, for once, want to be myself*". When he decided to take this bold step, he became *the Michael Jackson;* we all have come to acknowledge and that too without the support of Jackson 5.

Example: *Racism*

People are adjusting themselves for the happiness of others, let this adjustment be for traditions, friendships or love; But what they fail to realize, is that being the self, holds 80% of your natural power.

This stat has the capacity to go up to 100%, if you allow yourself to grow naturally.

Without being your real self, you would not know, what is meant for you and what is wrong for you.

Without being your real self, you would attract people, who are in love with your impersonation. Possibility is that you may push some people away in the process, since they may take you as immature.

Without being your real self, you may get approval of the people, but you would never get eternal satisfaction. Imitation would become your reality and you would eventually become frustrated of your surroundings,

A number of people have low self-esteem, as a result of which they do not like themselves, but they need to take a new start, in order to manifest in all the right ways.

Example: *Relationship*

Relationships are sacred. If I start a new relationship with a young girl, using blatant lies about my live; the relationship would not proceed in any direction. If I lie about my worth and about my possessions, she will soon come to know about my reality and would lose all the respect for me. Being honest and truthful in the relationship would help me to win her approval and her unconditional love. Moreover, the relationship would be smooth and uncomplicated.

Example: *Scientists and the Academics:*

Most scientists tell the truth, but many of them are liars, who present exaggerated facts, so as to draw the attention of the public towards them or to gain fame in the world of science.

Since they have presented an embellished piece of information and if it is an important discovery, it would soon become the part of academic books of the students. The new generations would learn from the lies, oblivious about the anomaly of the situation. Future scientist will have to dissect the truth, from the myths (starting all over again), instead on learning honestly from those before him/ or her, and then would take the torch ahead. A way of finding out Scientific Myths & Frauds is when a scientist quickly tries to sell his medicine and claims that it has been checked for all kinds of side effects. He claims that it is the best remedy for a fatal ailment and would provide relief to the patients from pain. Such aggravated claims with urgency to sell, must raise questions from the masses.

Bottom line of discussion: In order for us to grow immensely, it is important to thrive using the values of truth. Lies are temporary and they eventually reveal themselves. People spend their lives in a constant state of turmoil, using lies as their cover. The lies told my scientists hold the universe behind. All these anomalies in the system need to be removed and people must be truthful in their daily conduct. They should pass on the values of truthfulness to their children as well, so as to make this world a better place.

Scientific impression X: A formula of truthfulness for the scientists: Scientists must clear all the false doubts about previous discoveries and must reveal the fact with truth.

Truthfulness for adults: The adults must be truthful in their conduct since these values in turn would be passed on to their future generations.

All my teachings to the mankind are simple and easy to comprehend.

No special meditations, no glamour talk is required to know your true self. But only ways to conduct the self, the inner energy, and so much more, that is made simple, but makes you out to be the greatest of yourselves, as I also help those that guru special meditations, and stuff like that, by making such a beginning, so much easier on you, giving you the proper tools, and energetic tools, for any ride that life has to offer.

I want my students to pass on what they have learnt from me. They must not hold special sessions to past on knowledge, instead their conduct must be such that people would have a natural inclination to learn from them. When people would approve of your real-self, you would have a natural authority over them. I want you all to form teams of mentors and spread out in the world to pass on the light in the universe.

REMAIN BLESSED AND FOCUSED And I PRAY YOU ALL MAY DWELL IN TRANQUILITY:

All will soon find out the true sense, of value, towards One's own life; and will come to understand it. For it is then birthed, within that moment, of understanding, in which the subject will be able to balance themselves, with more control, over the outcomes, of One's own "NATURE".

The Proper AWARENESS:

Recognize, and observe all interests, along with well needed to be focused upon situations, and people. That this method will also help you to become more acknowledged, even about the self.

With this method, I advise you to use your own natural feel of patience, interest, along with the passion to do so, as needed. Which is the very passion to change things, know the truth about things, carrying out actions, in ways to succeed, (that are well understandable to you, quite naturally); in order to conduct/ make the self better at/ and to really gain true wisdom, about the self, (dealing with the intentions of your own physical acts, and verbal acts as a final choice being made, for self inner peace, and success in any situation involved with you.)

Making the proper adjustments for better outcomes, in any situation, is only a part of the endurance. Yet make sure that you are well-aware about the outcomes of your choices so that you can have personal and social satisfaction in the future.

All of the people, who would master the highest points of understanding, would find peace in nature and its ways. They would be able to comprehend the complexities associated with the situation, would be able to predict the outcome and would develop an inherent ability to shun the negativity. Doing an act and knowing its results is one part of the understanding; however, an ability to stand resolute in the face of consequences, without blaming or labelling someone else for your actions, depicts self-actualization. Comprehend the logic behind the "come around game" of the nature and be resolute to become a person dedicated for humanity.

"This will soon become a habit, through the practice, if interested".

Take this and use this with all that you practice, in life, to make outcomes as perfect as possible. That practice, with a passionate time being spent, will soon turn the guide of practice, into a habit well recognized.

Walkers's Definition of a habit- When something is being practiced, and/or exercised by the individual, so repeatedly, that the mind catches on to it without any doubt, nor speculation, from enough experience.

You must pay more attention, to situations that surround you, (also involving you ;) by using a natural interest, to do so, in a more natural way. You will have to sharpen your goals, around the truth it's self. "Like a flower stem, growing around a stick, to balance"

"HAVING A WORD WITH THE ENTIRE WORLD"

It is now time to fix the way we all have been living in this world. "Creating a domino effect of love and peace, that will last till the end of the world, is the ultimate objective here".

I've been planning on this for years now, on how I could do wonderful things for all of mankind (in both forms: natural and the supernatural). I don't plan on crying for what I want, but yet I would rather make it happen, for myself. I work through "Inevitability" and my plans are to help feed, shelter, cloth all individuals, and to teach you all the missing links, towards completion on a much more personal level, of the inevitable Laws of Nature.

The intention here is to gather all the people from varying states of the world, which have been divided due to hideous belief system, under the common banner of humanity. This would be done by using truth as a tool to mould the hearts of the people. People must realize that the divide on the basis of religion, culture, cast and creed if meaningless, since we all are humans and we all must get together to give back to the nature. Operate in the world, using the power of "recycling methods". These methods acclaim that a human must purify himself from all sort of negativities and in turn should re-use his new self to spread light of righteousness and positivity in the world.

Moreover, remember that you have to be good to the people, in order to have blessings for the future. However, if you want to avoid the wrath of Karma, I want to all to do this by following my method.

We all know, that you must do whatever it takes, in order to get to a certain point, in life(great or small); But it takes a proper mind state, to make things much more easier, on the self. Turning negative energy, from within (about a situation), into that positive energy, needed, by finding a solution, not wanting to do things the hard way, and using this fact, as a motivational tool ;(now keep this in mind) to get where you are going, much easier.

I would start by presenting a scenario to you. Imagine it is my first day at work and the job that I have joined requires hard labour. I will start off by getting acquainted with the place and the people, but as I make attempts to get familiar with the job, the time would pass by.

After I have got to know the people, I would then make attempts to know the nature of the Job, but since I have spent the major portion of my day, knowing the people around me, the genuine tine problems would arise. I would eventually get acquainted with the work and would get used to the culture of the organization. The next step would be to look forward for the opportunities of growth.

That was just an example, of using natural adaptation, as a tool source.

Natural Adaptation = Getting familiar with the basics, by becoming amateur first.(from the little experience offered, for you to gain or desired by you to have); and as the growth, you will become a bit better, at your skill,(hopefully mastering the basics, as your goal) throughout time.

Here the problem has worked as a tool to help us to look for solutions and the solutions have been utilized for personal gains and prosperity.

Now back to getting rid of Karma the simple way, without having to practice so many methods that you would have to master by deep passion. Here is a way to Master many situations, the simple way, without all of the extras. All you need is a deep enough passion, to make the changes. People are creating webinars, and stuff, on different forms of meditation, with created a created add-on, so that they can prosper from your money, for their time. Here it has been made simple.

Whenever you get rid of something that you do not want and want to get rid of it physically and emotionally, you'll begin to feel relieved. When you know that you have done something wrong,(in the past, or present) and the inner you is bothering you, about it(called guilt); it is then that the energy from it, will form guilt, and if guilt isn't corrected by acts of rejuvenation, or replacing such matters, it may very well become an influencing energy of ego. Now if you was to lie to the self, about the situation(which is denial, and denial is a lie) just to live with yourself, the rest of your life, trying to find better ways to look at the situation, rather than fix it, will only turn that energy into somewhat of a confused energy, a liable energy, that tags along, and brings great weight against the self being honestly relieved, from within.(within the mind, we must remember that knowing better, and knowing period has an energy that also triggers three folds in a more contract kind of way). So, instead of something coming back to you, based on what you've said or done, it goes more like

"*This is what you get, for knowing* better", but yet it is still for you to learn more from your mistakes, as you grow and go. The things that you do, and how you feel about those choices you've made,(in past and present times) brings about how you would judge the self, as being you.

What would be your approach towards something that is contradictory to your sets of belief? Once you have done something against your belief set, you would feel guilty and would not be able to forgive yourself. You may forget a portion of the thing that you have done wrong, but an active aura of energy would not let you forget everything. The guilt, along with the desire to blame yourself, would not allow you to forgive yourself. Now I will teach you how to break away, the simple way.

Having all of this information is good, but my explanation would have an in-depth meaning if I quote an experience here.

I would go step-by-step in answering the questions regarding the situation on hand.

Narrator: *So how would I become able enough to master such truths, about life, and their reality, (that is known, as well as the unknown)?*

Leroy Walker:

It would be best to find a strategy that would work best under all of these situations. Find a strategy, through self-actualization and by following my commands that would help you to spread the message of love in the world. Learn from your mistakes and give back to the people that you have learnt on your path in the pursuit of the truth. Once you are connected with the people on personal level, you would notice that people have come to acknowledge your efforts and you would soon have unconditional control over them.

"Time to see things through"

A person sets up his own reality and he must be well-aware of his personal needs and demands.

You all are the rulers of this Earth and therefore, I command you to stop abusing the nature and stop condemning your own people. Break away from the traditional ropes of cultural and sectarian differences, lift your eyes and search for the ultimate truth that would lighten up your soul and would have infinite benefits for your fellow humans. You all had been energies and you all had been altered into a physical form of flesh and blood since you have a purpose in life. Search for the ultimate goal in your lives, be resolute to follow your dreams and become the master of your own destiny. A human being has ultimate powers, since they are invincible, considering their determination and resolution to achieve their goals. So, ask yourself "what is my purpose is life? Why I have been created by God?" Once you have discovered the answers to these questions, work untiringly on the past of greater success.

"Give it to the man and it will come back. For the only help that man needs is to help himself"—Leroy Walker

In the next section, I would be providing

reasoning for the long-held sets of believes.

*You all had been sent down to this world for a specific purpose; let it be one purpose, or a number of purposes. Also, remember that your actions would dictate the outcomes and hence your future. If you learn from your mistakes, you will grow as a person, or the lesson would be lost.

This means that uncertainty would be a constant part of a man's life.

This also means that a person would add value in someone's life, since he has been sent down for a purpose.

It also means that we need to have faith in all human beings and should treat them equally. We need to have faith in ourselves for a better life ahead.

You were told that you were being asked before being sent into this world and you agreed to die after a certain period of time. If you do not agree with this theory then come and stand by me.

It is also commonly said that Adam and Eve ate the fruit of wisdom against the divine orders and the human beings of today's world would repent for their mistakes. If you think this theory is faulty, then come and stand by me.

It is being said that Lucifer was caste down from the Heavens, to the Earth, to live among humans. He has been labelled as a disobedient and cruel Angel and it is believed that those who follow him would be condemned by Lord. I want you all to know that God is all love and affection; he would not punish his creation with Lucifer, who is several times more powerful than humans.

If you do not support any of the above theories and belief that they have been suggested by humans, rather than the Almighty, then come and stand by me.

Man has been suggested by Almighty to see his high standards and to utilize the power of his contemplation to understand this world.

Man is equivalent to power and Authority on this world and therefore I have faith in all of you, since I am aware that you are capable of being your best selves,

Being able to stratify life, gives "Man" more meaning to One's self, as he become empowered by recognizing his number, "Which is the personal Calling, of all Man, of Any Kind"; which means that he must be treated as equal to everyone else.

Once you have understood the power of human as a distinct creation of God, I want to emphasize on the importance of self-worth once again. Live as a free bird and love the person, you want to love. Live your life to its fullest and choose a friend or a partner, which is closest to your heart. This should be your ultimate approach towards life and it would make you happy and content with yourself.

Another intriguing question that is often asked from me is; *what is the truth behind heaven and hell? Would I actually dwell in either heaven or hell?*

Answer: Human mind is powerful and once you die, it would be able to see in multiple dimensions. The power of your mind would increase by several multitudes once you die and it would thus create its own heaven or hell, depending upon its past experiences. The religion has fooled many of its followers into believing in physical hell or heaven. The concept of physical heaven and hell was taught to the humans in order to monitor their morality and to keep them away from wrong-doings and sins. In reality, any desirable place is heaven and any unwanted place is hell for a human mind. Human mind has a power to dream and once we die, we would enter a in a mental state of imaginable heaven or hell, depending upon our expectations. The idea of physical heaven and hell keeps a person under a continuous trauma of 'ifs' and 'what ifs', which they need to escape as soon as possible. You must know that Heaven is filled with imaginable happiness, love and food; whereas, hell is the product of your fear and guilt. Therefore, I would suggest you to have complete control over your thoughts and respect Nature and the cycle that has been set-up by nature.

"Getting along as a one World"

To live under a single banner of humanity, I suggest you all to respect, share and love one another. Cast a positive influence on your fellow humans and be a precedence of best of your kind.

The best way to keep positive towards live and even towards your enemy is to harness love and happiness and ward-off all kinds of negativities. Negativity is a waste of time and attracts wrath of the nature. Long held negative energy would yield deceitfulness and hatred among people.

Once people would observe an aura of positivity attach to you and would recognize your efforts towards the betterment of humanity, they would come to respect you and would become you loyal followers.

My message here to all of you is of respect and mutual love. Do not only respect others but respect yourself and stay from evil acts of envy, jealousy and ignorance. When you would respect others with all your heart, it would eventually become your habit and passion. Once you treat people with reverence, they would return your compassion with the same multitude and you would soon hold a special place in their hearts.

"The Pathway towards Becoming a master":

A person, who is dedicated to the cause of self-awareness, is truthful and is resolute to learn and practice the acts of righteousness, would soon find himself on the path of spirituality. He would eventually become a genius and would be able to become a master for the rest of the world.

"RESTORING YOUR INNOCENTS"

"In order to overcome a problem, you must find a solution; because it is within the solution, that one would come to find peace over misery."—Leroy Walker

Let us take an example in this regard. You are a gruesome killer and you have killed an innocent person. The guilt would take over you and you would not be able to get detached from the misery of your Karma. The best way to handle this pain is to do something for an innocent person to get rid of the cursing of your Karma.

I tell you right now, that I have the remedy against Karma by this Universe and the universe has a reason to provide me with this solution. The reason is that the nature wants me to pass it on to all of you for your betterment and welfare. I believe that every human being must get a chance to restore their innocence before their deaths and that no human being must leave this world, unless their innocence has been restored.

The tool for success is to admit your evil act and make a resolution to do a positive act of similar multitude so as to get rid of your guilt.

To the Killer- If you had committed such a crime, to be honest with you, I'm here to help you get it right, no matter what the situation maybe, and no matter from which so ever caste or creed you are from. It is now time for "you" to not beg in one sense, for forgiveness, while remaining guilty in another; yet you will find out a way, or ways towards forgiving yourself, in order for you to get some sort of relief, just to know that you've been saved, from a certain type of problem, some kind of way, and that this way be the only way intended by any Godly source, that symbolizes the true nature of righteous acts, genuine love, happiness, and togetherness.

Now you may think that it is hard to forgive one's self, or maybe you feel like you are not in the perfect shape to forgive yourself, hoping to be redeemed by your traditional idol. However, no matter what you do, if you do not do anything for it, you will not become genuinely redeemed, do to you not gaining that redeemed energy that is needed for the ride. Now you just may be asking yourself this question i.e. "*How do I gain that redeemed energy needed, that would purposely help to get rid of my hidden guilt(s), and guilt(s) alike?*" well I'm here to tell you that if redeeming acts are not employed by you, redemption will not be some-what believed to the fullest, and if such acts upon redemption is not intended by you, then you would only be of hope(as in hoping for such a relief, hoping that God had forgiven you) without the proper actions to follow, for reason. The religions have sacred difficulties associated with them, so as to be redeemed by the religion; you have to repent from the religious idols or from the relatives of the deceased, as the case may be in case of a certain religion

Now let me ask you a question, *how would you realize that you have finally been forgiven*? Well just like seeing gives the full energy upon believing, you must perform such a virtuous act that it must break you off from guilt.

While you are using this restorative tool, your energies, fuelled by your hopes may pick on you in a while, with its "what ifs scenarios". *These what if scenarios would pose questions like "What if I have already been forgiven and I do not need to repent anymore?"*

You must remember that if you would not repent with all your might and with all your heart and would not perform a good act of equal multitude, the internal guilt would prevail and would snatch away your peace of heart. By only performing a genuine act of kindness would provide you with an opportunity to get rid of your guilt.

Yet again, if you was to find a way to restore your own innocents, if done the right way (through acts)

no matter what the case may be, you would feel the weight of guilt being left-away from your soul and mind. This negativity would then begin to leave you, if you repent in the best possible manner, by doing a genuine act of kindness.

This not only shows strength, but also ways to obtain it, dealing with redeeming the self, breaking away from bad karma, destroying negative thoughts about the self, of past acts, which had burdened the mind, and perhaps the soul. It is then that you will not have to run away from such a denial, for denial is a lie. Yet if you were to ever dwell on the past, for future reference, you will not have to suppress your memories. You would not have to live with your lie and hence would be able to live and survive freely.

Once acts are being performed by you, to replace those that are of the past (being negative) with that being of good natures, devoting the self to such positive actions, throughout the time, that would out number, and out balance the pressure of such past; that this would indeed release you from the past, by you knowing for certain that for the life you had taken away, you shall and will come to save many.

It is important for you to recognize that you can repent for your foul act, but you must not make attempts to forget it, since you may not repeat it in future. If your crime is big enough that you need to repent for it, then it would be intense and hence should not be forgotten. If you forget that you have committed a crime, it would depict your insensitivity as a human being. You need to repent so that you may be able to confront yourself in the future. You need to feel guilty for your foul act so that you can give back to the nature, what you have taken away from it. Moreover, the guilt would keep you away from possible chances of crime in the future.

Once you have exercised and understood the art of dealing with your Karma, you would become to cherish happiness and would master the art of imparting it to others. The pursuit of happiness demands the filtration of negative energy from your lives and working with good intentions for the welfare of the humanity. Once a person is a prisoner of his guilt and the victim of his Karma, he must put in all kinds of efforts to bring in positivity in the world and to impart happiness to the people of this universe. The repentance in this manner must continue until he feels that he has been finally forgiven.

When the Nature would observe the efforts that you are putting in to wash-off the dirty stains of misconduct, it would draw new patterns of well-being and happiness for you. If this book helps you to get rid of your guilt, I suggest you to pass on the message for the welfare of entire humanity.

To the Killer, you must devote yourself some kind

of way towards saving lives, and it is for you to strive on becoming the reason for lives alike, to change for the better. Teach them how to restore the self, and so forth. Help one another, and it is for you to remember that I love you forgive you, and it is now that you must do the work upon forgiving yourselves.

To the thief, robber and liar – I suggest you to find a way to give back to the universe, which would completely nullify the effect of your crimes in the past

Find and read (in this book), about the "Angels of The Light" organization that would soon surface. This would be a major worldwide program, inviting the humanitarians to work for the betterment of societies.

Once you have joined this organization, you would be greeted wholeheartedly by me and the Angels and your journey towards perfect self-perfection would commence almost immediately. Since now you know about my organization, named "The Angels", I request you to visit our Facebook page and notice the efforts of my Angels for the restoration of nature. You would be able to realize that the efforts put in are genuine and are free of charges. Our objective is to serve all nations and to provide them with free shelter, clothing and food. I have a commitment with nature to ward-off evil from the universe and let the eternal peace swell here.

A Moment Dedicated for Poetry:

"Pestilence"- (Which is a sickness of the Earth)
How long will the pain last to my enemies glad?,
Well once no more tears, after death, might I add;
Doctors have no cure for a sickness like mine,
This plague allowed by fate, for only "It" can hide;
Knowing by the river lays the evil creatures,
Acknowledging life problems, growing intense;
Which my life had been poisoned, what's next I am to mention?
That now I have seen "The Lamb", and all of his intentions...
Even though I am sick, and almost final,
"HE" giveth unto me- "The Seed", of everlasting Survival!!!

His Loyalty is rich,
His Justice is powerful,
His Love is the truth,
And his faith is never doubtful!!!
Even though I'm sick, my values speak loud!,
For I am a child, of Good Natures,
And not just another child...

I've gotten another day to live, another day to sleep;

Happy for when tomorrow comes,
So I can be at Peace...

Now the hour comes,
And my fears had been swept away,
For I ought to go out, as a "Knight",
That it is now, I've seen the King's face.- (Leroy)
Thank you World, and Guardian, of ours,
Thanks for sending me, one of the greatest men,
of all times!

Amen- Amen.(Death)

"Famine"

As the plagues stare within us, and our children,
No hospital, with no chances in life, means no
living!

And no means, of the Beast, means home
invasions, without equal;
Which had now been promoted by the greediest
and grimiest hearts, of all people...
As We All Sit Back,(impatiently), waiting on a
relief.

No acceptance, of the New World, means no offerings, till the death, of you;

Yet the teachings of each other, is really all, what we have left, for you!

Learning how to eat, from a dead Carcass,

turning fruits into wine,

watching out for water moccasins-"Somewhat, like the Indian Tribes".

No house, no cars, no lies, but yet- we still have no food,(by far);

So look down upon us,(all other great countries),

Because "Here", is where "We Are!"

Homes being raided, as the hunger is being created,

Love is still being made, but what type of love is there, to aid it?

Majority of us will fade away, from the lack, of traditional foods;

But sometimes, it's what's, already, around us,

That is of need, to be used.

Starving the needy, for those that are of "GREED",

Killing us slowly, with the lack of all "FEEDS".

Bleeding from the mouth,(vomiting, from the stomach);

laughing out louder, because the hard part is almost over!!!

You may rule money, stores, and many of Great Needs,

But Leroy has the Greatest Offering,

Dealing with the greatest of needs, for All Things...

Laughing out louder, laughing all the way, to "death";

Without any worries

JUST KNOWING--- That my children will be left, behind, with one of the greatest kings ever!!!

----------------(DEATH)----------------

(Leroy) Speaks;

People of the land, I have come;

Not only have I come, but I have come in peace.

Now it is for you to come to me;

Now rejoice, and eat...

"Warfare"

The good of nature is so in reach, for each and every woman and man;

That religious empires had now created similar yet

diabolical plans (as the gunfire rings amongst all the people)...

One mind, with one finger, on the trigger, with many demons, creating many enemies, for closure;
Yet listening to the soldier scream "Get back on the ground!", with a face set for a killer;
Just lying over the hand that had just been blown to pieces.

(Whoa!!!) > Boom, Boom, Boom, Boom, Boom!!!
(Watch out!!!) > Bang, Bang, Bang, Bang!!!

Guns smoke, and explosions; open raw flesh, (deceased and exposed)
Warfare is now being held all across the lands of the world...

"ABOUT THE AUTHOR"

Leroy Walker spent the major portion of his life in Demopolis Alabama and had a hard time growing up. The hardships in his life did not make him rigid and unpleasant; instead his heart was filled with the love of humanity. He wanted to serve the humanity by connecting with them at a personal level. Leroy managed to have very few friends, since he had a resonant personality with unique and distinctive perspectives.

The Author here has spoken for himself.

"I am not a member of any secret society!

I am not wasting my time by supporting a certain hidden agenda, nor do I have any veiled religious motives. I am not a Maudi, nor an Imam, neither Jesus and nor God. I have been assigned a duty by the nature, which is to take care of humanity and to serve them with the best of my abilities.

When I say I am not a part of any secret society, it means that I do not follow their schools of thought. If any of the societies would request me to support their cause in future, I would refuse it to them, since my only duty is to take care of this world.

I am only a young man, who is aware of the needs of this world and want to make some valuable contributions for the betterment of all of the nations of the world.

I am not an attention-seeker, neither a fan of fame. My motto is to impart the message of peace and to gain personal satisfaction from it. I would define myself as an ordinary man, with an extra-ordinary gift. Universe has bestowed me with its secrets and I have chosen this book as a medium to share the wisdom of the Nature with the people of the world.

I am not a follower of any religion. My ultimate source of peace is to strive for the welfare of humanity and to serve the needy people of this world. I am a humanitarian and my name is Leroy Walker.

This is all that I have to say about me. Please do not truth any other piece of information that you receive about me, since I am only an exceptional man with a dedicated personality and a giving-heart, always ready to serve humanity. I am not an egoistic person and therefore, I would always like to connect with my followers at a more personal level. I am humble when I talk to people and the universe has taught me the art of treating people with care and respect/ I am well-aware of my actions and the motive behind it is nothing, but to see peace dwell in this world. My name is Leroy Walker and I send my *earnest regards and warm wishes to you all."*

I would make further attempts to gain knowledge that would help me to serve humanity in a more pragmatic and meticulous manner.

My life has taught me that the key to change is to strive for it, to recognize it and to embrace it for the betterment of self and of the society. If you would only recognize the problems in your surroundings, they are pound to proliferate and grow; but if you the problems would be perceived as changes in the circumstances and would be approached in a decisive manner, the world would become a better place- Leroy Walker.